Contemporary

BEACH
HOUSES

Down Under

Stephen Crafti

Published in Australia in 2008 by
The Images Publishing Group Pty Ltd
ABN 89 059 734 431
6 Bastow Place, Mulgrave, Victoria 3170, Australia
Tel: +61 3 9561 5544 Fax: +61 3 9561 4860
books@imagespublishing.com
www.imagespublishing.com

Copyright © The Images Publishing Group Pty Ltd 2008
The Images Publishing Group Reference Number: 804

National Library of Australia Cataloguing-in-Publication entry:

Author:	Crafti, Stephen, 1959 –
Title:	Contemporary beach houses down under / Stephen Crafti.
ISBN:	9781864703009 (hbk.)
Subjects:	Vacation homes – Australia – Pictorial works.
	Vacation homes – New Zealand – Pictorial works.
	Seaside architecture – Australia – Pictorial works.
	Seaside architecture – New Zealand – Pictorial works.
	Architecture, Modern.
Dewey Number:	728.72

Coordinating editor: Robyn Beaver

Designed by The Graphic Image Studio Pty Ltd, Mulgrave, Australia
www.tgis.com.au

Pre-publishing services by Splitting Image Colour Studio Pty Ltd, Australia
Printed by Everbest Printing Co. Ltd., in Hong Kong/China

IMAGES has included on its website a page for special notices in relation to this and our other publications.
Please visit www.imagespublishing.com.

Contents

8 Introduction
by Stephen Crafti

12 A Great Beach House
Studio 101 Architects

18 Site Specific
Ashton Raggatt McDougall

24 Geometrical Wonder
McBride Charles Ryan

28 Enveloped in Colour
Hayne Wadley Architects

32 A Cedar Container
JAM Architects

38 A Black Lighthouse
Bellemo & Cat

44 Leap of Faith
Jackson Clements Burrows Architects

52 Private Views
Wolveridge Architects

56 The Beach Studio
Bird de la Coeur Architects

62 Grafted
Chenchow Little Pty Ltd

68 Designed for the Future
Bark Design Architects

74 A Celebration of Timber
Cox Rayner Architects

78 Time Out
Daniela Simon Architect @ SODAA

82 Tower House
Lahz Nimmo Architects

88 A Canopy of Tea Trees
Paul Morgan Architects

94 Sleepy Hollow
Woods Bagot

102 Connecting to the Sea
Wright Feldhusen Architects

108 The Main Course
ITN Architects

112 1950s Simplicity
BKK Architects

116 Views of Swan Bay
JAM Architects

120 Timber Lantern
Bark Design Architects

126 Amid the Moonahs
Richard Kerr Architecture Pty Ltd

132 Prefab Views
BURO Architecture + Interiors

136 The Sands
Robert Andary Architecture

138 In Context
Swaney Draper Architects

142 Designed to Last
Swaney Draper Architects

148 Lang Cove
Bailey Architects

152 Zigzagging Along the Coast
Casey Brown Architecture

158 A Great Opportunity
SJB Architects

164 Designed from Afar
Daniel Marshall Architect

168 The Colour of Tea-trees
Marcus O'Reilly Architects

172 Blue Sky and Ocean
Odden Rodrigues Architects

180 Reaching for the Sun
Strachan Group Architects

184 A Growing Family
Bernard Seeber Architects

190 On a Ridge
Sorensen Architects

194 Pacific Views
Architektur

202 Designed for Two or Four
Centrum Architects

208 Bed and Breakfast
Architect Leigh Woolley

212 A Touch of the South Pacific
Walter Barda Design

220 Turned Around
Phorm Architecture + Design

224 A New Life
Studio 101 Architects

232 The Letter K
Ashton Raggatt McDougall

238 Glimpses of Water
Luigi Rosselli Architects

244 Controlling the Views
B.E. Architecture

248 Orua Bay
Moller Architects

254 Balinese Influence
Bligh Voller Nield Architecture

262 Tropical Treehouse
Carr Design Group

268 Alfresco Living
Hulena Architects

274 High on a Hill
Iredale Pedersen Hook Architects

280 Nestled in the Dunes
Kerstin Thompson Architects

284 Architect contact details

288 Acknowledgments

Introduction

This is my fourth book showcasing architect-designed beach houses in Australia and New Zealand. Why the fascination with beach houses? Was it childhood vacations spent on the coast, or simply memories of happy times at the local beach? As a child growing up in Brighton, a bayside suburb of Melbourne, I spent endless days lazing on the sand and running in and out of the water. But these things aside, I've always regarded the beach and the sea as liberating environments, places that draw you away from the rituals of everyday life.

While the experience of 'getting away' is a key driver of these books, so is the opportunity to discover great architecture along the coast. Away from the restrictions of building in a city, coastal locations offer architects a means of escape, a place to create challenging designs. There are fewer council restrictions, heritage overlays and neighbours' objections to contend with in designing a beach house. And there isn't the same level of concern about 'what it will mean for property values in the area'.

As lot sizes are generally greater outside the metropolitan area, and the landscape denser, the 'new kid on the block' is allowed to explore the coastal site. Some of the beach houses featured in this book can be seen from the road. However, many homes are nestled in the scrub, their form only emerging as the car winds its way along a dirt driveway. An angular roof perched above tea-trees offers the first sign of a house. Alternatively, a wall made of rusted steel conceals a large three-storey house on a steep site.

Beach houses have come a long way since the fibro-cement shacks of the 1950s. While the coast is still dotted with these gems, new beach houses tend to be considerably larger and more sophisticated. Some may still have fibro-cement walls, but there's usually no outdoor bathroom or wash house. While the contemporary beach house has moved on, thankfully there are elements from the past, such as informal living areas, timber floors, large decks and outdoor showers, that continue to be incorporated.

This book presents a selection of beach houses that offer not only an escape, but something new. What are the elements that make a truly memorable beach house? Is it the architecture and the way it captures our imagination? Or is it the smaller, simpler things, such as large picture windows that magnify the gnarled scrub and the sand dunes?

Each of the houses featured in this book offers new ways of looking at the coastal environment. One house, 'The Letter K', by Ashton Raggatt McDougall Architects is a long way from the 'shy' beach house, concealed under a rock. With its sharp angular walls and roofline, it is as brave as a person entering the sea during the winter months. This beach house also offers

some insight into the clients, a couple interested in exploring architectural concepts as much as the coastal setting.

Other featured houses are more introverted. A house designed by Swaney Draper Architects ('Designed to Last') is more traditional in form. With a stone spine wall and clad in stained timber, this beach house is quite restrained. Other houses integrate the past with the present. Architect Bernard Seeber extended a modest timber bungalow in Perth by adding a substantial new wing made from steel ('A Growing Family'). While the two periods are considerably different, there is a dialogue between the old and new.

Some of the houses in this book draw on experiences from holidays spent abroad. Interpreted in a uniquely Australian or New Zealand way, these homes may include generous loggias or palm-filled courtyards. At Whale Beach, on Sydney's northern beaches, is a house designed by architect Walter Barda ('A Touch of the South Pacific'). The owners of this house lived in Brazil for several years. Their brief to Barda included a reminder of those times, without being derivative of another place or time. As a result, the house has a rustic, worn-in look, with recycled timber on the exterior and the interior.

Architect Peter Woolard, from Studio 101 Architects, also used recycled materials for a house he designed at Lorne, Victoria ('A Great Beach House'). Not only are some of the materials reused, but so are many of the original walls of the home. The 1960s ground-floor footprint was retained and a second level added. The house now benefits from water views and also caters for a family and regular guests.

Some of the changes in today's beach houses have been instigated by changing patterns in city homes. Like city homes, beach houses now regularly feature two distinct living areas, one for adults, the other for children. In Studio 101 Architects' Lorne house, a second living area for the grown-up children takes the form of a refurbished garage, complete with kitchenette, bathroom and built-in banquette-style beds. This accommodation is not only used by the owner's children, but also by the children's friends.

Many of the featured beach houses demonstrate subtle differences in how people live in their weekenders or holiday homes. Kitchens, for example, take a more prominent position in living areas, with the act of food preparation and shared meals central to the holiday experience. In the city, the kitchen is as much about concealing the evidence of food, with the scullery often tucked away.

Outdoor terraces and balconies also appear in many of these beach homes, as do floor-to-ceiling glass doors and windows that take advantage of the sea views. And even when a sheltered outdoor nook is required for wind protection, architects create a sense of transparency through the house to ensure views from every vantage point.

Some of the finest beach houses aren't simply about 'looks', but are designed to enhance the experience of living on the coast. Swaney Draper's beach house at Lorne is filled with the sound of crashing surf. As memorable is the sound of bird and animal life scurrying around a house at Blairgowrie, Victoria, designed by Kerstin Thompson Architects ('Nestled in the Dunes').

Regardless of the size of these beach houses, there is an overriding desire for low-maintenance homes. Timber can be left to weather, or materials such as Rheinzink allowed to dull over time, avoiding the need to repaint a house every few years. The beach house isn't guaranteed against wear, but it's generally designed to age gracefully, with as little human assistance as possible. Along with the empty nesters wanting to spend more time at the beach than in the city, many young families are also beach house owners. Younger owners might have more energy to deal with maintenance issues, but they value time spent with their families.

Some of the beach houses in this book show the lengths to which people go to purchase the right parcel of land and successfully build on it. Jackson Clements Burrows Architects, for example, managed to build a house on an extremely difficult slope by first designing a concrete retaining wall ('Leap of Faith'). Resembling a tree house, the house occupies a small footprint on an impossibly steep site. Another house, designed by SJB Architects, overcame numerous challenges ('A Great Opportunity'). The steep site had languished on the market, with most prospective buyers putting the vacant land in the 'too difficult' basket. However, with ingenuity and the right design, SJB was able to successfully build an enviable home.

As land prices in the city increase, a large home in the suburbs isn't always attainable. However, a smaller home (house or apartment) combined with a beach house is becoming a significant trend for some families. For empty nesters as well as younger people seeking an escape from the city, the beach house is becoming the new 'dream home'.

Stephen Crafti

A Great Beach House

STUDIO 101 ARCHITECTS

'We didn't want the house to interfere with the vegetation or the natural watercourses on site.'

There were few meetings required to determine the design of this beach house, in Lorne, Victoria. The clients, a couple based in Noosa, responded to the architect's emails, as well as the occasional phone-call. 'The brief was essentially to "design a great beach house",' says architect Peter Woolard, director of Studio 101 Architects.

Rather than create a solid mass on the steep site (falling approximately 10 metres towards the street), Studio 101 Architects designed a lightweight structure. Conceived as two pavilions, supported by steel beams, the cypress-clad beach house appears to float above the property. 'We didn't want the house to interfere with the vegetation or the natural watercourses on site,' says Woolard, pointing out the space under the house to allow water to pass. 'The house was also elevated to allow for natural ventilation, benefiting from the sea breezes,' he adds.

Woolard designed the two pavilions with the living pavilion 'slipping' past the sleeping pavilion. The entry point acts as a breezeway. Framed with a timber and glass door on one side and a floor-to-ceiling glass louvred window on the other, the irregular shaped lobby is an interstitial space. 'When the door and louvres are open, you feel as though you're sitting on a verandah,' says Woolard, who also used the entrance to separate the living areas from the three bedrooms.

The main kitchen and living areas are defined by a change in level, one of five in the house. The changes in level are only slight, but they allow for a journey through the house rather than one direct path to the water ahead. 'In a sense the two pavilions have been cranked on the site to enliven the experiences,' says Woolard.

A small viewing platform leads from the lounge. From the kitchen, a more internalised deck is protected from behind by the second pavilion. 'We've still maintained the view of the sea. But we were also conscious of providing an outdoor space that could be used. The winds down here can be fairly strong and unpredictable,' says Woolard.

While the house can be likened to a suitcase (opened up on arrival), the design is considerably more complicated. It may appear as a simple beach house but in reality the house has been finely crafted to the site and oriented to fully benefit from the path of the sun as well as the sea views.

Photography by Trevor Mein

1   Entry porch
2   Entry
3   External decking
4   Kitchen
5   Dining
6   Living
7   Balcony
8   Master bedroom
9   Robe
10 Ensuite
11 Passageway
12 Bathrom
13 Laundry
14 Rear entry stair
15 Bedroom 2
16 Bedroom 3

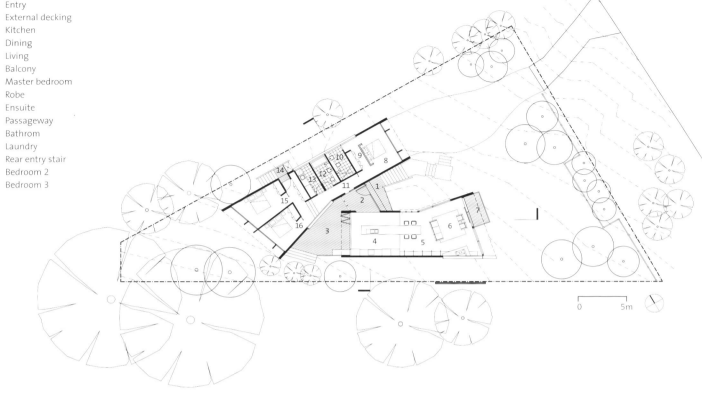

Site Specific

'It's quite an organic design. There's a plasticity to it, where the walls and ceilings have been moulded.'

This house on Victoria's Westernport Bay is surrounded by 80-year-old banksias, with views of the ocean directly ahead. Designed by Ashton Raggatt McDougall (ARM), the original plans for a new house centred on the panoramic vista, with typically large picture windows. However, to preserve the banksias, as well as respect the sensitive sand dune setting, ARM subsequently decided to take a different approach. 'We wanted to create a more understated quality,' says architect Ian McDougall, a director of the practice.

The owners, a couple with three children, wanted a place that would be a refuge. They also wanted a place that was fairly communal. 'They're a musical family and it was important for them to come together and perform, whether piano or violin,' says McDougall.

As the site has a fall of approximately 7 metres to the beach, the house was positioned close to the road, to maximise the views and minimise disruption of the vegetation. An uncovered deck at the front of the house is used for parking, with the front door approached indirectly via an extended deck. 'It's not a classical approach,' says McDougall, referring to the off-centre position of the front door.

Past the threshold, a more expansive view of the site is offered. Stained black cedar cladding acts as an important frame to the house, as do extensive decks that wrap around the upper level. Internal plywood walls and ceilings, which appear to have been cranked into position, set up views of the bay. 'It's quite an organic design. There's a plasticity to it, where the walls and ceilings have been moulded,' says McDougall, pointing out the different ceiling heights in the open-plan kitchen and living areas.

Part of ARM's brief included creating a reasonable distance between the parents' and children's bedrooms. As a result, the parents' bedroom, including a walk-in dressing area and ensuite, is located on the top level, while the three children's bedrooms, bathroom and separate play area are located below. But rather than both levels being symmetrical, the lower level has its own setbacks, in line with the trees on the property. 'We were determined to retain all the established banksias on the site. The irony was one of the largest banksias blew over in a storm after the foundations were laid,' says McDougall.

Photography by John Gollings

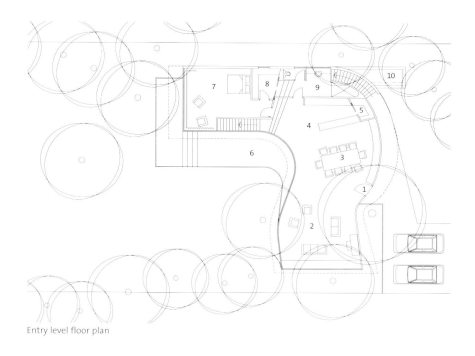

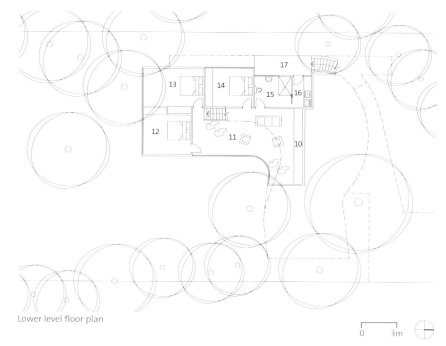

Entry level floor plan

Lower level floor plan

0   3m

1	Entry	7	Bedroom 1	13	Bedroom 2
2	Living	8	Dressing	14	Bedroom 3
3	Dining	9	Bathroom	15	Bathroom
4	Kitchen	10	Store	16	Laundry
5	Pantry	11	Family	17	Deck
6	Deck	12	Bedroom 4		

Geometrical Wonder

M c B r i d e   C h a r l e s   R y a n

'We wanted to evoke a sense of the fibro cement beach shacks in the area. We didn't want to make the house feel too precious.'

The owners of this beach house were after something completely different from their city home, a traditional Californian Bungalow. Located in Rye, on Victoria's Mornington Peninsula, the house designed by McBride Charles Ryan (MCR) Architects couldn't be more dissimilar.

Designed for a couple with three children, the house was partially inspired by the 'Klein Bottle', a model of a surface developed by German 19th-century mathematician Felix Klein. 'In principal, it's like a doughnut. You can twist and distort it, but it will only change topographically if it's cut. In a sense, there's no beginning or end,' says architect Rob McBride, who worked closely with his partner, interior designer Debbie-Lyn Ryan.

The house is made of compressed cement sheets with a black metal roof, which folds down in part to form an external wall. Moonah trees, with gnarled blackened trunks, anchor the house to the steeply sloping site. 'We wanted to evoke a sense of the fibro cement beach shacks in the area. We didn't want to make the house feel too precious,' says McBride. A front door, clad in cork, not only creates an unusual entrance, but also alludes to a cork stuck in a bottle.

When the 'cork' is removed, a bright red staircase and walls appear, like liquid solidified around an irregular-shaped lightwell. The entry lobby and laundry are at ground level. And although not apparent from the front façade, there's camouflaged back door providing access to a central courtyard.

There are no distinct separate levels; instead the rooms splay off the staircase around the central void. As you ascend the staircase there is a large flexible space that functions as a rumpus room and extra room for the children's friends to stay over. Continuing up there are two additional bedrooms and two bathrooms.

To maximise the light, as well as the views over the trees, the open-plan kitchen and living areas are located at the termination of the staircase, as is the main bedroom, a few steps above the living areas. Like the façade, the ceilings fold around the spaces like origami; likewise the fireplace, which appears 'folded' in one corner of the room.

The brief to MCR was for a joyous house, one that liberated the senses. And like a great party, where the bottle is left uncorked, the front door is regularly open to extended family and friends.

Photography by John Gollings

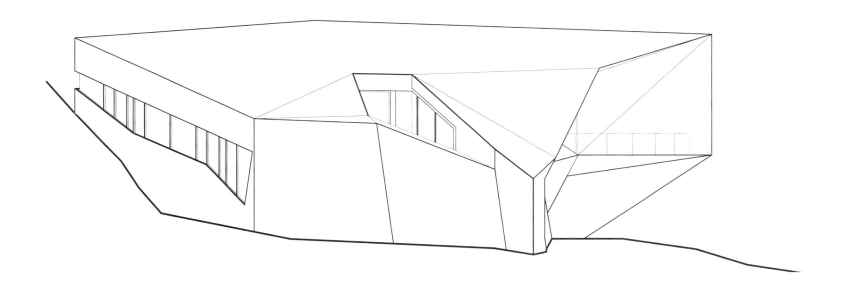

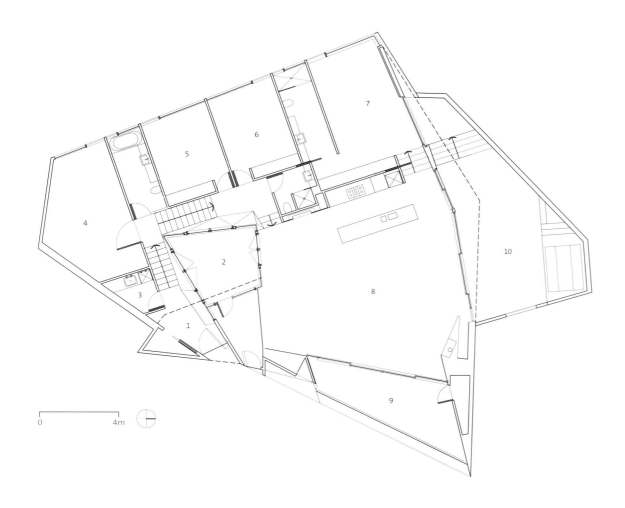

1 Foyer
2 Courtyard
3 Laundry
4 Rumpus
5 Bedroom 1
6 Bedroom 2
7 Master bedroom
8 Living/dining
9 East deck
10 North deck

0   4m

Enveloped in Colour

H A Y N E   W A D L E Y   A R C H I T E C T S

'We saw the helix as a way of binding and protecting the house from the elements.'

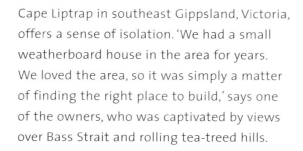

Cape Liptrap in southeast Gippsland, Victoria, offers a sense of isolation. 'We had a small weatherboard house in the area for years. We loved the area, so it was simply a matter of finding the right place to build,' says one of the owners, who was captivated by views over Bass Strait and rolling tea-treed hills.

Hayne Wadley Architects, who designed the new house, were likewise impressed with the unique surrounds. 'It's not a typical beach aspect, with surf and breaking waves,' says architect Andrew Hayne, who designed the house with his partner Katherine Wadley.

The brief to the architects was fairly simple. 'The clients wanted a fairly modest house, approximately 250 square metres including the separate guest quarters, with one large combined kitchen and living area,' says Hayne, who manipulated the design to fit between two stands of tea-trees. The architect couple were also mindful of creating a form that would provide some resistance to the prevailing winds.

As a result, the house turns its back on the point of entry with the concrete block façade featuring only highlight windows. The main feature upon arrival is a vibrant red steel and aluminium helix wrapping around the house. 'We saw the helix (a spiral shape) as a way of binding and protecting the house from the elements,' says Hayne.

In contrast to the southern elevation, the entire northern aspect features floor-to-ceiling windows. Combined with a large deck and broad timber staircase, the northern elevation loosely takes the form of a grandstand. A considerably more curvaceous line appears in the black Colorbond roof that encloses the main bedroom and the west end of the house.

While the palette of materials and finishes is relatively simple, the architects were keen to activate the interior rather than create a passive backdrop to the 'theatre' in front. As a consequence, a curvaceous plywood wall in the main bedroom wraps around and is expressed in the living room wall. 'There is that sense of being enveloped. It's a unique location and we wanted to make the interior reflect that,' says Hayne.

Photography by John Gollings

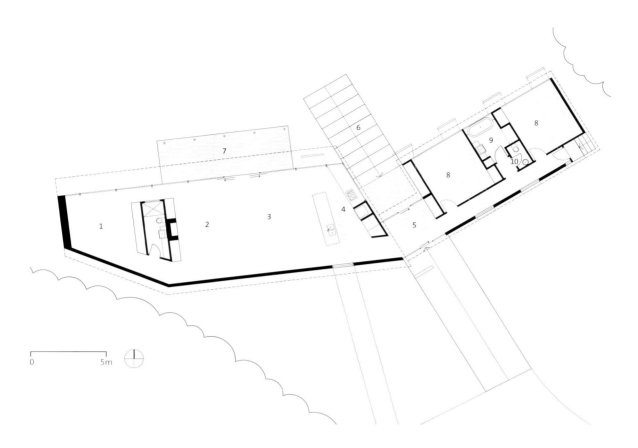

1 Master bedroom
2 Living
3 Dining
4 Kitchen
5 Entry
6 Viewing stairs
7 Deck
8 Bedroom
9 Bathroom
10 WC

0   5m

A Cedar Container

J A M   A R C H I T E C T S

'An important part of the brief was one large living space, whether for family or entertaining friends. '

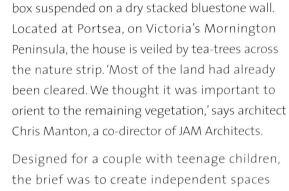

This house takes the form of a cantilevered cedar box suspended on a dry stacked bluestone wall. Located at Portsea, on Victoria's Mornington Peninsula, the house is veiled by tea-trees across the nature strip. 'Most of the land had already been cleared. We thought it was important to orient to the remaining vegetation,' says architect Chris Manton, a co-director of JAM Architects.

Designed for a couple with teenage children, the brief was to create independent spaces for both parents and children. As a result, the ground floor comprises two bedrooms and a guest bedroom, a laundry and a bathroom, together with a large rumpus room with its own kitchenette. 'It's a self-sufficient area. The children can invite friends over to stay and occupy the entire ground floor. Alternatively, the parents can close off the ground floor and simply use the upstairs spaces,' says Manton, who compares the design to a container, quickly opened upon arrival and as quickly shut down on departure.

While the brief included two independent zones, the owners didn't want the ground floor and first floor to feel as though they were two independent apartments. As a consequence, a double-storey void in the entrance links the two floors, as does a graphic timber staircase. And while one set of treads can be viewed from the front garden, the other set is concealed behind a seraphic glass and timber screen, creating a silhouette of moving people.

In contrast to the bedrooms downstairs, which are quite cavernous, the open-plan living areas on the first floor are bathed in light. While the light is generous, so is the volume – 3.5-metre ceiling heights over an expansive 12-metre-long room. 'An important part of the brief was one large living space, whether for family or entertaining friends,' says Manton. And although the living and dining area is expansive, it has been carefully delineated with furniture, such as a module lounge and dining table seating ten.

While floor-to-ceiling glass windows and doors to the outdoor deck and pool could have sufficed, the architects were mindful of creating protection from the harsher sunlight. Deep cedar blade walls and eaves frame the doors and windows, creating a sense of depth to this façade. 'Eventually the cedar will turn silver, not dissimilar to the trunks of these trees,' says Manton, pointing out gnarled forms through the elongated kitchen window.

The cedar and rendered walls are evocative of a beach house, as are the timber sleepers that surround the home. Used to define paths, as well as creating retaining walls, each sleeper is embedded with barnacles, shells and rusted steel bolts originally from an old pier. 'They were found in a recycle yard,' says Manton, who appreciates the added texture they bring to the design. 'The house isn't precious. It's about arriving, throwing off your shoes and enjoying the feel of timber under your feet,' he adds.

Photography by Gerard Warrener and Sharyn Cairns

Ground floor plan

First floor plan

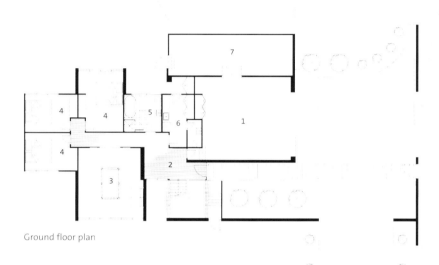

1	Garage	8	Study
2	Lobby	9	Void
3	Rumpus	10	Kitchen
4	Bedroom	11	Dining
5	Bathroom	12	Living
6	Laundry	13	Deck
7	Store	14	Pool

A Black Lighthouse

BELLEMO & CAT

'Black intensifies the landscape.'

A 1950s fibro shack once stood on this site at Point Lonsdale, on Victoria's Bellarine Peninsula. While the house was too small for the owners, a couple with two children, there were elements they fondly recalled. 'The typical beach shack of that period featured under-cover car parking. It was something they were keen to have in the new house,' says architect Michael Bellemo, a director of Bellemo & Cat.

The new house, of approximately 230 square metres, was conceived as two structures, connected by a large deck. 'Our clients wanted a separate study that could also double as a retreat, either for parents or when the children are older,' says Bellemo, whose inspiration for this structure came from a black lighthouse at Queenscliff, a historic town a few kilometres away. The 7-metre-tall study/retreat could also be compared to Australian bush hero Ned Kelly's helmet, with a picture window framing gnarled tea-trees.

The primary form of the house is rectilinear. The main bedroom and ensuite are located at the front of the house, cantilevered over the carport. The main living areas, including the kitchen and dining areas, are at the centre, creating a buffer between the children's bedrooms and informal living area to the rear. A floor-to-ceiling lime-green door separates the two living areas.

The home's north and west elevations are clad in sugar gum timber, stained black. In contrast, the south and east elevations have been finished with fibro cement sheeting and painted in a leaf-green colour. 'Black intensifies the landscape,' says Bellemo, who was also keen to create a link to the past by using fibro cement.

Although the site was relatively undisturbed during construction, an established acacia was removed from the front garden as it was blocking the entrance. In memory of the tree, Bellemo & Cat infused the design with a variety of green hues. An awning made of polycarbonate was designed with computer-generated images of leaves. Memories of the tree are also captured in the glazed bricks used in the fireplace, separating the living and dining areas. 'We're not trying to replace the tree. But it's important to make connections to the past,' says Bellemo.

Photography by Mark Munro

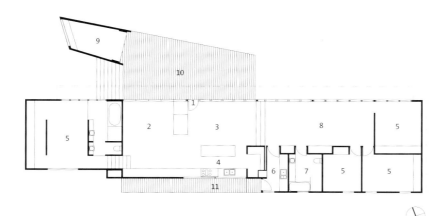

1 Entrance
2 Dining
3 Lounge
4 Kitchen
5 Bedroom
6 Laundry
7 Bathroom
8 Children's play room
9 Retreat
10 Deck
11 Ramp

Leap of Faith

JACKSON CLEMENTS BURROWS ARCHITECTS

'We wanted to capture the entire vista over Port Phillip Bay.'

The owners of this house took a leap of faith in accepting the initial sketches presented to them. Resembling a burnt-out log, the house features a 9-metre-long cantilevered wing. 'We wanted to capture the entire vista over Port Phillip Bay,' says architect Jon Clements, a director of Jackson Clements Burrows (JCB) Architects.

The form of the house evokes a log, or two branches, when both wings of the house are seen in profile. JCB considered several aspects of the property, located at Cape Schanck, on Victoria's Mornington Peninsula. One of the strongest images was of an old campfire on the property, left with a burnt log.

Using one of the covered dunes as an anchoring point, the house extends in two directions. One wing comprises the kitchen and living areas, while the other, with the main bedroom, ensuite and study, is perpendicular to these spaces. Supporting these two wings is a plinth-like base, containing two guest bedrooms, a bathroom and second living area. 'The owners were fairly open when it came to the brief. They didn't mind the log analogy. But they wanted the "log" to rest at one level,' says Clements. 'When they (a semi-retired couple) come down on their own, there's no need for them to go downstairs,' he adds.

JCB could have designed an all-concrete house, given the area's predisposition for bushfires. However, with a 50-metre clearance around the house, the architects were able to explore the use of timber. Fire-hardy timbers such as spotted gum were used to clad the steel-and-timber-framed house. 'We've stained the timber black. It picks up the trunks of the tea-trees,' says Clements, who used cedar for the windows and sliding glass doors.

While the house appears relatively exposed, the front door is at the end of a winding driveway at the top of the hill, discreetly placed next to the garage. Past the front door, the expansive living areas take in dramatic views over Bass Strait, Point Nepean and Port Phillip Bay. The only distraction to the main vista is the large deck and swimming pool, adjacent to the kitchen and dining areas.

The palette of materials used in the kitchen and living areas shows different aspects of the hollowed form. The graphic black and white kitchen was treated like a cube, with joinery appearing to be carved from a solid form. In contrast, the lounge area features warmer materials such as spotted gum around the fireplace and a cedar-lined wall. 'The cedar has a warm feel about it. It's like the fleshy parts of the timber that haven't been burnt,' says Clements.

Photography by John Gollings

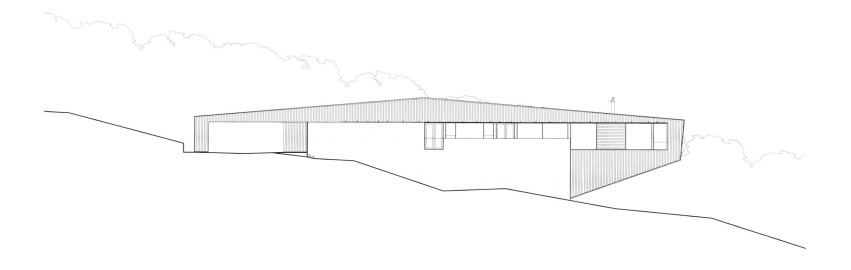

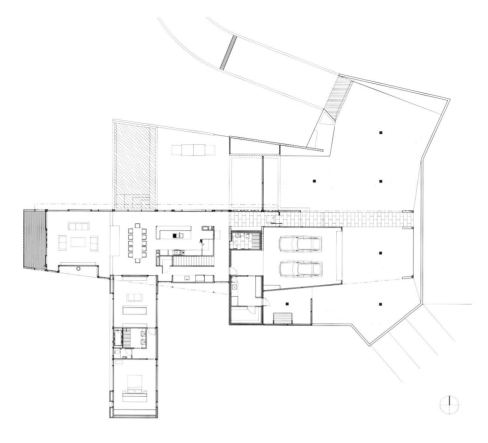

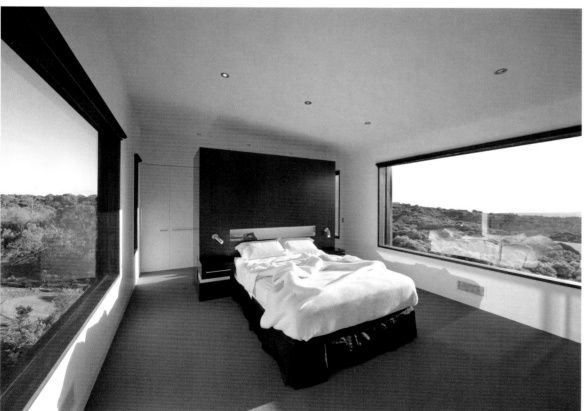

Private Views

WOLVERIDGE ARCHITECTS

'We wanted to use materials that were resilient in coastal environments.'

This beach house occupies a fairly exposed site at Sorrento, on Victoria's Mornington Peninsula. Surrounded by cottages, the 800-square-metre site originally contained a 1930s timber bungalow and numerous mature cypress trees. 'The trees completely overshadowed the site. Whatever light came into the house was diminished by the home's small-paned windows,' says architect Jeremy Wolveridge.

The house, built for a couple with adult children and grandchildren, was designed to accommodate an extended family. 'The brief required four bedrooms, with the grandchildren's bedrooms and play area at a reasonable distance from the main bedroom,' recalls Wolveridge. 'They also wanted privacy from the street'.

In contrast to the pitched tiled roofs of surrounding homes, the form and materials used for this home are strong and contemporary. A 5.5-metre-high Corten steel box creates a landmark on the corner. This rusted steel cube is juxtaposed by the home's double garage, clad in Western red cedar and stained ebony. 'We wanted to use materials that were resilient in coastal environments,' says Wolveridge, who also used cedar to clad the side and rear elevations. The materials also help in differentiating the functions within the home. Three of the bedrooms, including the main bedroom are clad in cedar, while the children's bathroom is essentially clad in stone.

In contrast to the enclosed crate-like appearance of the side elevation, the home's rear northern aspect is open and light-filled. Large glass doors lead from the main kitchen, living and dining area to a large deck, with a freestanding fireplace and built-in barbeque. And it's only from the back garden that the dramatic cantilevered canopy can be fully appreciated. Framed by highlight windows, the canopy appears to float above the living areas. It was important to recognise the private areas of the house while strengthening the connection between the indoor and outdoor areas.

Although there are large public gestures made to the street, there are smaller thoughtful details that can be appreciated from within. The ceiling over the main corridor, for example, features timber battens below a polycarbonate roof. 'This allows filtered light into the core of the house,' says Wolveridge, who sees the corridor as a separation point between the kitchen and living areas. And while the kitchen was designed as a box within a larger volume, it was also treated as integral to the living areas. A window seat in the living area also features a polycarbonate roof, allowing light, rather than views of the neighbouring home, to enter.

Photography by Derek Swalwell

1	Entry	11	Robe
2	Hallway	12	Bedroom 2
3	Kitchen	13	Bathroom 1
4	Dining	14	Bedroom 3
5	Living	15	Bathroom 2
6	Living deck	16	Bedroom 4
7	Lap pool	17	Entry deck
8	Ensuite	18	Garage
9	Bedroom 1	19	Laundry
10	Study	20	Private court

The Beach Studio

B I R D   D E   L A   C O E U R   A R C H I T E C T S

'We wanted people to stop and pause and admire the blue gum.'

Researching a garden shed was the starting point for this beach house on Victoria's Mornington Peninsula. Instead of being tucked away in the back garden, the shed became the focal point of the house. 'Our clients wanted a painter's studio/workshop. They also wanted guest accommodation,' says architect Vanessa Bird, a director of Bird de la Coeur Architects. Instead of locating a shed in one corner and adding another rarely used bedroom, the two were cleverly combined to form a larger structure in the front garden.

Made of cedar, like the house, the two interconnecting forms were oriented to maximise views towards three established eucalypts. The studio also features a cedar screen, with views of the sea, and a pacing balcony, a requisite for every artist. Complete with built-in timber seat, it's one of the many private nooks favoured by the owner.

The outbuilding forms a covered walkway leading to the front door. Past the pool and shed, the path is terminated by a curved ramp. Forming part of the entry to the house, the ramp doubles as lounge seating. 'We wanted people to stop and pause and admire the blue gum,' says Bird, who directed the curved façade towards the impressive branches.

The dimensions inside the house are substantial, with the kitchen, living and dining areas forming one large continuous space. Oriented to the pool and manicured lawns, the living areas have been carefully aligned to the views. With deep reveres doubling as window seating, both indoor and outdoor, there's a relaxed ambience to these spaces. Even the barbeque isn't relegated to the backyard, with the kitchen bench extending out to the deck for alfresco dining.

While the living areas, with 4-metre-high ceilings, are generous, the dining area is defined by a timber canopy. Concealing skylights as well as ventilation slots, the canopy creates a sense of enclosure. The adjoining kitchen can also be fully enclosed by means of timber sliding doors that disappear into structural columns. 'There are times you don't want the kitchen on show, particularly if you're having guests for dinner,' says Bird.

An elevated study above the main living areas screens any noise to the bedrooms. 'It was conceived as a large platform,' says Bird, who was keen to create a variety of spaces that could be used in different ways by the whole family.

Photography by Shannon McGrath

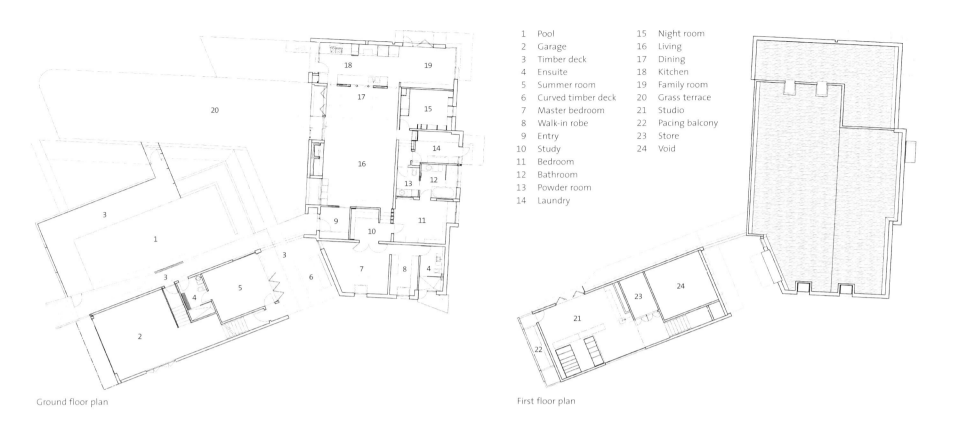

1 Pool	15 Night room
2 Garage	16 Living
3 Timber deck	17 Dining
4 Ensuite	18 Kitchen
5 Summer room	19 Family room
6 Curved timber deck	20 Grass terrace
7 Master bedroom	21 Studio
8 Walk-in robe	22 Pacing balcony
9 Entry	23 Store
10 Study	24 Void
11 Bedroom	
12 Bathroom	
13 Powder room	
14 Laundry	

Ground floor plan

First floor plan

Grafted

C H E N C H O W   L I T T L E   P T Y   L T D

'*It's not supposed to be clear what
is inside and what is outside.*'

This beach house was originally built at the turn of the 19th century. A semi-detached home on a long narrow site, it needed major alterations and additions. 'Retaining the two-storey home wouldn't have given our clients what they wanted,' says architect Tony Chenchow.

The site, which slopes dramatically towards the Pacific Ocean, required a design that would embrace the view. However, while the original Arts & Crafts-style house wouldn't achieve this, the architects retained the ground floor of the original house. They also retained the home's original sandstone walls, but 'grafted' on a contemporary second storey. Constructed in steel, glass and fibro cement and encased with aluminium louvres, the first floor cantilevers above the sandstone plinth.

The ground floor was restored and reconfigured. Three bedrooms occupy the original structure, while a new main bedroom, ensuite and deck were added to the rear. As the first floor is entirely new, the architects were able to design around a view. 'You're not aware of the ocean as you cross the bridge (leading from the garage to the front door). It's only when you enter that you can see the entire vista,' says Chenchow. As the street is on the high side, one enters at the first floor.

Chenchow Little's design features a series of verandahs, decks and courtyards. A long corridor, linking the kitchen and living areas is akin to a

breezeway with aluminium external louvres. 'It's not supposed to be clear what is inside and what is outside,' says Chenchow, who worked closely with co-director Stephanie Little. 'The louvres are fundamental to the design. We wanted to protect the house from the harsh light. We also wanted to ensure privacy from a neighbouring home,' says Chenchow.

The first-floor spaces are loosely defined from the courtyard and decks. The front room, used as a family room/office has a large sliding door leading from the breezeway. 'The room can be closed off, but it's generally left open to attract the sea breezes,' says Chenchow. The dining and living areas at the rear of the home are also flexible. Glass sliding doors frame this space on three sides, one of which leads to a covered deck, the other deck being roofless. 'The wind here can get fairly strong. We wanted to ensure the outdoor areas could be used for most of the year,' says Chenchow, who was also keen to ensure views to the ocean from the central courtyard and kitchen.

The house has many features associated more with an inner-city warehouse than a house near the beach. 'When you're inside, you're not aware of neighbours. The focus is directly towards the water,' says Chenchow.

Photography by John Gollings

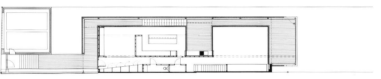

First floor plan

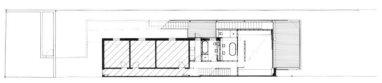

Ground floor plan

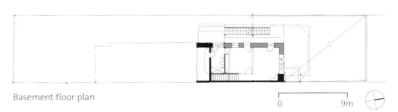

Basement floor plan

0   9m

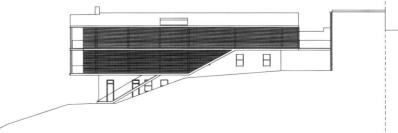

Designed for the Future

B A R K   D E S I G N   A R C H I T E C T S

'We didn't want to create a new house that looked as if it had just arrived.'

This beach house was designed for a retired couple. 'They wanted a house they could stay in for the long term,' says architect Stephen Guthrie, a co-director of Bark Design Architects.

Located in Old Tewantin, a ten-minute drive from Noosa, the house is only a short stroll from Noosa River. The relatively compact site – approximately 500 square metres – is surrounded by fishing shacks and timber bungalows. 'We didn't want to create a new house that looked as if it had just arrived,' says Guthrie, who clad the house in Western red cedar chamfer boards, limed to create a weathered look.

The courtyard-style house is located near three of its boundaries and is essentially oriented to the sunlight and a large street tree. Although the house doesn't have views of the canal, it does enjoy views over the lap pool in the front garden. Elevated above the ground and indenting the home's façade, the pool is enjoyed while approaching the front door. 'There's something quite magical about running your hands over water,' says Guthrie.

The open-plan kitchen, dining and living areas, defined by a change of ceiling heights, are on the ground floor. The kitchen and living areas feature 2.5-metre-high ceilings, while the dining area benefits from ceilings that are almost 5 metres high. 'We wanted to create a sense of intimacy in the living area,' says Guthrie, who included a large deck off this space.

Although the house was designed for a couple, there are three bedrooms, two of which are located upstairs, linked by a bridge/corridor that also doubles as a mezzanine-style study. The third bedroom, located adjacent to the lounge on the ground floor, is like a self-contained apartment. A kitchenette, as well as an ensuite, allows this room to be used by family or friends. 'This room was an important part of the brief. Our clients didn't want to negotiate stairs in their latter years,' says Guthrie.

Photography by Patrick Oberem and David Sandison

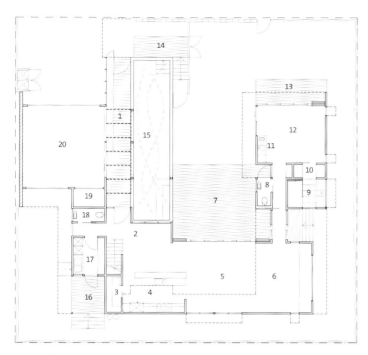

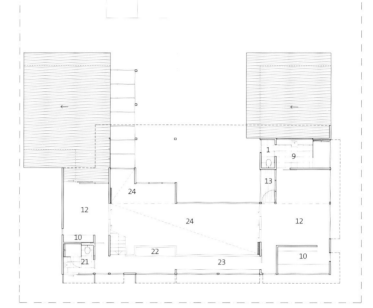

1 Entry boardwalk
2 Entry
3 Pantry
4 Kitchen
5 Dining
6 Living
7 Living deck
8 Powder room
9 Ensuite
10 Robe
11 Kitchenette
12 Bedroom
13 Bedroom deck
14 Pool deck
15 Swimming pool
16 Drying deck
17 Laundry
18 Powder room
19 Store
20 Carport
21 Bathroom
22 Study
23 Library
24 Void below

Ground floor plan

First floor plan

A Celebration of Timber

COX RAYNER ARCHITECTS

'We wanted to make sure the outdoor space was used.'

Elysium is a unique concept in Australian architecture. Conceived as a totally architect-designed estate, it brings together some of the country's leading and emerging architects. A short drive from Noosa, the only brief to architects by the developer was to ensure every house was different.

This house was one of the first to be completed on the estate. 'We wanted to celebrate the use of timber. It seemed appropriate being on the edge of conservation parklands,' says architect Rebekah Vallance, who worked closely with her husband, architect Casey Vallance, and architect Michael Rayner, director of the practice.

The house is almost entirely made of Australian hardwoods such as spotted gum. Timber battened screens and minimal windows in the front façade prevent harsher light entering the home, as well as creating privacy (at the end of a cul-de-sac). Past the front door, the house opens up to a north-facing courtyard and pool. 'The entrance is quite protective. We wanted a slow introduction to the house,' says Rebekah Valance, pointing to the spotted timber gum on walls extending to ceilings. The timber screen framing the staircase provides an abstract reference to the strong verticality of the adjacent eucalypt forest.

The main living areas, with the formal lounge and dining area separated by the kitchen, are on the ground floor. The kitchen protrudes out to the terrace, also clad in timber. The extensive use of timber ties the house to its bushland setting with careful detailing emphasising the house's crafted quality.

Upstairs are three bedrooms and bathrooms, including a large main bedroom and ensuite. A media room leads to a Juliet-style balcony that pierces the central void over the staircase. 'It's a relatively large house for the site (approximately 500 square metres). To avoid an underutilised 'backyard', the intent was to create a seamless transition from interior to exterior, to ensure the outdoor living area was integral.

The northern terrace of this house acts as an indoor/outdoor room. The double-height space is protected from sunlight in two ways: via a translucent roof and by a tier of timber battens acting as a canopy. While there is a beach nearby, this house draws its strongest reference from the adjacent nature setting, creating an elegant beach retreat.

Photography by Christopher Frederick Jones

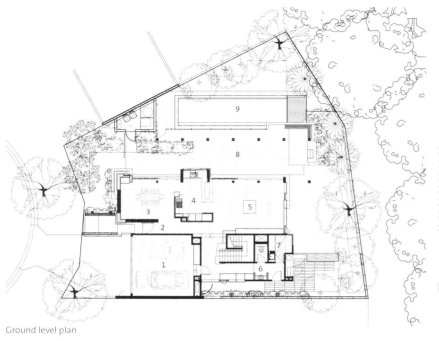

1 Garage
2 Entry
3 Dining
4 Kitchen
5 Living
6 Powder room
7 Laundry
8 Loggia
9 Pool
10 Family/media
11 Bedroom 2
12 Bathroom
13 Bedroom 3
14 Walk-in robe
15 Bedroom 1
16 Ensuite

Ground level plan

Upper level plan

Time Out

D A N I E L A   S I M O N   A R C H I T E C T   @   S O D A A

'*I refer to it as "luxurious camping". It's a place to protect you from the wind and cold.*'

Architect Daniela Simon wasn't looking to build a beach house for herself. 'But then a friend bought a block of land here. Even as I was driving down, I had no intention of buying,' says Simon, who couldn't see the point of travelling 530 kilometres south of Perth on a regular basis. However, when she visited the coastal heathland, it wasn't long until she signed a contract.

Situated on 4 hectares of land and adjacent to her friend's property, this house at Bremer Bay is next to the Fitzgerald River National Park. 'It's a ten-minute walk to the beach and only a short drive to the nearest township, Bremer Bay,' says Simon, who designed the house for her partner and three adult children. 'The children come down with us as well as independently,' she adds.

While Simon's initial thoughts were that she wouldn't use a beach house, she now regularly uses it. 'It's like paradise. It gives me a complete break from the city,' she says.

The house is relatively modest in scale. Approximately 140 square metres, it is conceived as an alternative to camping. 'I refer to it as "luxurious camping". It's a place to protect you from the wind and cold,' says Simon. Made of rammed earth and Corten steel, the split-level house was designed to accommodate as few as two and up to ten people. There are two enclosed bedrooms. And there are also beds on the mezzanine above the living room and in the living room itself. 'I wanted the design to be flexible. There's something quite special about curling up and going to sleep in the corner of a living room,' says Simon, pointing out a nook in the living room that extends beyond the walls.

Rammed earth appears on the exterior of the house and is expressed in the interior walls, including the kitchen. Rather than the usual red colour associated with rammed earth, these walls are grey. 'I combined the rammed earth with cement. I wanted the exterior walls in particular to disappear into the landscape,' says Simon.

Photography by Robert Frith

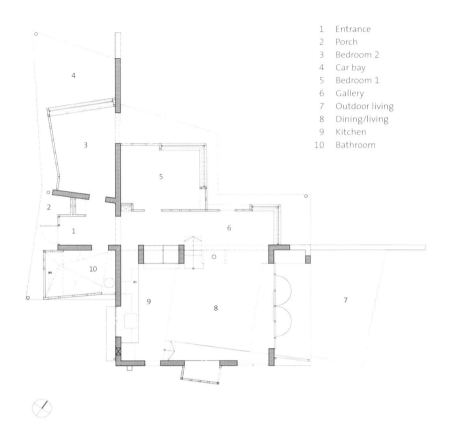

1   Entrance
2   Porch
3   Bedroom 2
4   Car bay
5   Bedroom 1
6   Gallery
7   Outdoor living
8   Dining/living
9   Kitchen
10 Bathroom

Tower House

L A H Z   N I M M O   A R C H I T E C T S

'People know it as the tower house. And they're keen to stay there. It's become a landmark building.'

This beach house at Casuarina Beach is only an hour's drive from Brisbane airport. Located in northern New South Wales, the position attracted the owner, an American working in Singapore. 'Our client was looking for a place he could occasionally use. He also wanted a house that he could rent out,' says architect Andrew Nimmo, a co-director of Lahz Nimmo Architects.

Casuarina Beach has undergone a significant transformation in the last few years. Once a sand mine, the land was purchased by developers who reinstated the sand dunes and subdivided the land for housing and commercial facilities. This house is located on the highest point of the area.

The 'tower' concept formed part of the client's brief. 'He saw it like having a tree-house,' says Nimmo, who initially tried to persuade his client to think again. 'Towers aren't often used, with access being one of the problems,' he adds. However, as a rental proposition, as well as a home, the tower has proved successful. 'People know it as the tower house. And they're keen to stay there. It's become a landmark building,' says Nimmo. Another request from the client was to include a self-contained bedroom. 'He wanted a room that he could stay in, even if it was for just a night'.

While the house appears relatively large from the street, it is actually quite compact. On the ground floor are two bedrooms and a bathroom, together with a double-height entry foyer. One of the bedrooms on the ground floor was designated as a 'bunk room', designed to accommodate several beds, or alternatively could be divided into two, further down the track.

Upstairs are the kitchen, dining and living areas, with a stairwell leading from the living area to the tower. The external staircase, enclosed with timber battens, appears almost to have been 'clipped on' to the house. The house is made of ivory concrete block work, rough-sawn plywood and fibro cement.

One of the most used parts of the house is the large deck separating the main bedroom from the kitchen and dining area. 'It's the coolest place in the house. You get all the sea breezes. It's also protected (by a roof) from the sun,' says Nimmo. 'It enjoys the finest views, with the dunes on one side and the swimming pool on the other,' he adds.

Photography by Brett Boardman

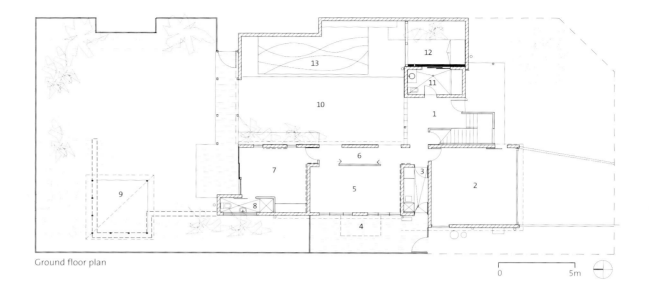

Ground floor plan

0   5m

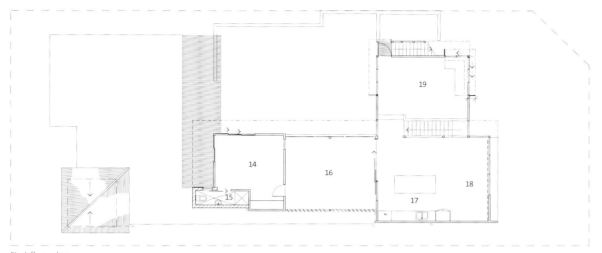

First floor plan

1   Entry
2   Carport
3   Laundry
4   Drying
5   Bunk bedroom
6   Hall
7   Bedroom 2
8   Ensuite 2
9   Garden pavilion
10   Courtyard
11   Bathroom
12   Bathroom courtyard
13   Pool
14   Bedroom 1
15   Ensuite 1
16   Outdoor room
17   Kitchen
18   Dining
19   Living

A Canopy of Tea-Trees

PAUL MORGAN ARCHITECTS

'I suppose you could say it was aerodynamic in shape. It's an expression of the strong wind forces down here.'

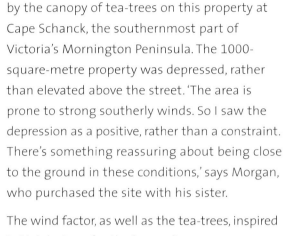

Architect Paul Morgan was initially captivated by the canopy of tea-trees on this property at Cape Schanck, the southernmost part of Victoria's Mornington Peninsula. The 1000-square-metre property was depressed, rather than elevated above the street. 'The area is prone to strong southerly winds. So I saw the depression as a positive, rather than a constraint. There's something reassuring about being close to the ground in these conditions,' says Morgan, who purchased the site with his sister.

The wind factor, as well as the tea-trees, inspired initial designs for the house. 'I suppose you could say it's aerodynamic in shape, an expression of the strong wind forces down here,' says Morgan, who used glass, plywood cladding stained walnut brown and composite aluminium panels for the exterior finishes. 'I didn't want to use materials that would detract from the tea-trees,' he adds.

One of the most striking aspects of the open-plan living area is the bulbous water tank. Made of steel and painted white, it collects rainwater from the roof, with the overflow directed to an external tank. While the tank replaces the traditional fireplace as the focal point of the room, it's an important reminder of Australia's drought conditions over the last decade. 'The tank also acts as a structural

support, as well as cooling the room,' says Morgan. The tank divides the living area into four distinct parts: the kitchen, living areas, dining area and a flexible space.

Like the organic-shaped tank, the kitchen bench and joinery is fluid in form. Made from laminate and vinyl, the kitchen appears integral rather than separate to the living areas. Handles were concealed on the kitchen joinery to ensure a seamless connection; the unusual cement pavers used for the flooring in the kitchen and living areas are a combination of hexagon and pentagon-shaped tiles.

In contrast to many new beach houses, this one is relatively compact – approximately 135 square metres (with an additional 40 square metres of outdoor decking). 'The house was designed for two families. I'm there about three days of the week. My sister will also be using it,' says Morgan, who sees the working week becoming more flexible. 'There's no longer the strong division between work and leisure there used to be. Cape Schanck is only an hour and a half from Melbourne. Many people spend that amount of time commuting,' he adds.

Photography by Peter Bennetts

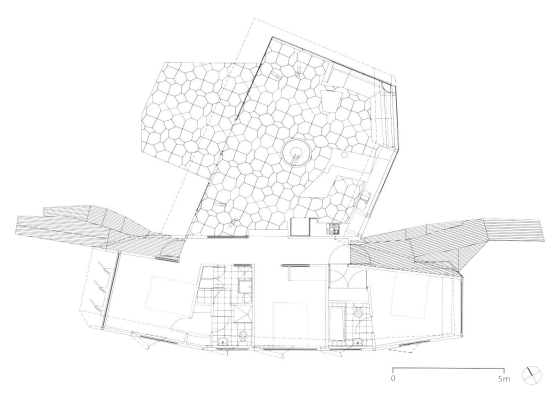

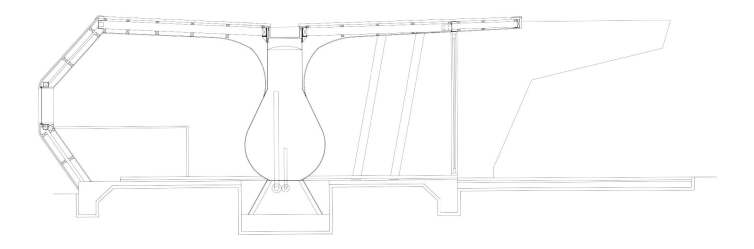

Sleepy Hollow

W O O D S   B A G O T

'*The brief was for a house with a sense of permanence, rather than the temporary.*'

Point Leo, on Victoria's Mornington Peninsula, is a small coastal enclave, comprising little more than 30 houses. However, for those fortunate few, it offers everything from a surf beach to walks along the coast. 'You feel like you're part of a community,' says architect Rodger Dalling, Managing Director Australia of Woods Bagot. Dalling, who has his own beach house at Point Leo, was delighted when friends asked him to design theirs.

The clients, a couple with three children, had owned a small fisherman's cottage on the site for 15 years. However, with a view to spending more time at Point Leo and less time in Melbourne, the idea of building a new house emerged. 'The brief was for a house with a sense of permanence, rather than the temporary. They also wanted something that was comfortable, and a house they could eventually retire to,' says Dalling, who worked on the project with interior designer Libby Thorton.

The occasional Force 9 gale winds at Point Leo also suggested a substantial home. Woods Bagot achieved this sense of permanence by using three materials, steel, glass and rammed earth. The steel carried with it the farm vernacular (farmland abuts the property) and the rammed earth, with its sandy texture, evoked a sense of the beach. 'We wanted to express these materials in the house,' says Dalling, who juxtaposed the steel and rammed earth at various points.

The house was conceived almost as two pavilions slipping past each other. The bedroom pavilion, constructed in ribbed steel, is box-like, alluding to a farm shed. This wing contains three bedrooms at ground level. The main bedroom, ensuite, dressing area and storeroom are on the first level. The bedroom pavilion is linked to the kitchen and living wing via an enclosed breezeway. With a glass roof and views at either end of the passage, one can experience the elements without feeling the full effect.

The kitchen and living areas occupy the other pavilion. The large open-plan kitchen and living areas are simply defined by a towering Corten rusted pillar and fireplace (6 metres high) as well as by changes in ceiling heights, including a double-height void over the dining area. Above these areas is a large mezzanine study and second living area. As with both living areas, decks surrounding the house are used by the entire family. 'They tend to be used according to the position of the sun,' says Dalling, who deliberately created a non-specific front or rear to the house. Likewise, there are no fences or gates surrounding the property. 'People know everyone down here. And why would you fence off this view anyway,' says Dalling, pointing out the views over Westernport Bay and the coastal banksia park directly ahead.

Photography by Tony Miller

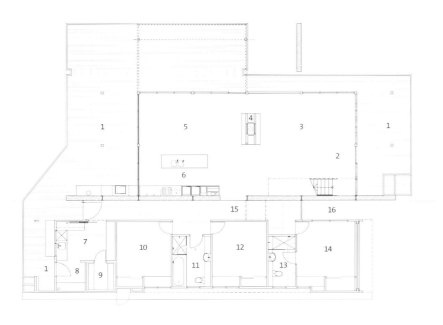

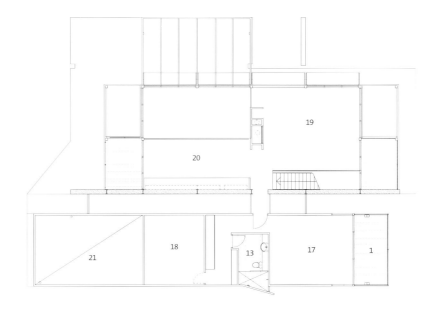

1	Deck	8	Store/mud room	15	Gallery
2	Entry	9	Cellar/wine store	16	Garden bed
3	Living	10	Bedroom 2	17	Master bedroom
4	Wood store	11	Bathroom	18	Store
5	Dining	12	Bedroom 3	19	Living
6	Kitchen	13	Ensuite	20	Study
7	Laundry	14	Bedroom 4	21	Roof space

Connecting to the Sea

WRIGHT FELDHUSEN ARCHITECTS

'You feel as though you're swimming out to sea.'

This house appears to merge with the sea. 'Our client is a keen swimmer. He wanted to be connected to the water, whether he was doing laps or relaxing inside,' says architect Tim Wright.

While the house enjoys 180-degree views of the water, there are houses directly in front. But as the house is perched on a hill, with a 6-metre fall of land from front to back, the vista isn't compromised by neighbouring homes. Relatively modest in size, the 500-square-metre site was subdivided by the owners. 'Split down the centre, two new houses enjoy unimpeded views,' says Wright.

Designed for a couple with two young children, the house is spread across three levels. Car parking and servicing equipment for the pool are at basement level. The kitchen, living and dining areas, a children's rumpus room, plus a guest bedroom and ensuite are on the first floor. On the second and top level are the main bedroom, dressing area and ensuite, as well as the children's bedrooms and laundry. As the site slopes towards the street, the laundry is aligned to ground level. Whether you're in the main bedroom or in the living areas, water can be enjoyed from most vantage points. 'Our clients wanted the house to be as transparent as possible,' says Wright.

To achieve this transparency, the house features extensive use of glass. Zinc cladding and off-form concrete also make up the range of materials used. Zinc, being a non-ferrous material, resists rust (essential being so close to the sea). 'The off-form concrete was poured to appear as though it had grown out of the site,' says Wright, pointing out the horizontal bands of concrete that form the base of the house, as well as in the walls of the double-height void enclosing the staircase. 'Our clients wanted a house that was low maintenance. But the house is fairly exposed, so concrete anchors the house to the site,' says Wright.

One of the most pleasurable activities for the owners of the house is using the pool, either for laps, or just for splashing in. 'You feel as though you're swimming out to sea,' says Wright, who cantilevered the main bedroom approximately 2 metres to strengthen the connection between house and water. 'It's only a rocky outcrop below. So the pleasure of the beach comes from gazing out through these windows,' he adds.

Photography by Olivia Reeves

Upper floor plan

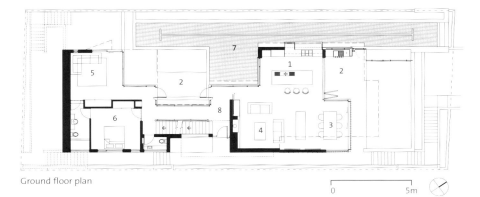

Ground floor plan

0   5m

1 Kitchen
2 Terrace
3 Dining
4 Lounge
5 Play room
6 Guest
7 Pool
8 Entry
9 Master bedroom
10 Walk-in-robe
11 Ensuite
12 Study
13 Balcony
14 Gallery
15 Bedroom 2
16 Bedroom 3
17 Laundry
18 Bathroom

The Main Course

I T N   A R C H I T E C T S

'They didn't want their city home reproduced down the coast.'

ITN Architects designed an entrée-sized beach house for clients at St Andrews Beach, on the southern tip of Victoria's Mornington Peninsula. The initial house, approximately 28 square metres (now used as guest quarters), was designed as an interim measure while the owners saved up to build something larger. 'The first house feels more like a caravan,' says architect Aidan Halloran, a director of the practice.

The brief was for a considerably larger house for the owners and their three young children. 'But like the first house, they wanted something that was informal, simple and robust,' says Halloran. 'They didn't want their city home reproduced down the coast,' he adds.

As the site falls away dramatically from the road, the house appears as a single storey from the street. The entrance and first floor are accessed from a bridge. 'You're not really aware of the lower storey until you reach the bridge,' says Halloran, who placed the second house approximately 7 metres away from the initial home. 'Most people like to sleep in. We didn't think guests would appreciate being woken up early with noise from the children,' he says.

In keeping with the owners' brief, the materials used for the house are relatively modest. The house is clad in silvertop ash, as well as Ecoply. And to ensure privacy, the front façade features only highlight windows. 'That's why it's been called the "fortress house",' says Halloran.

Past the front door, the house is considerably more open. The kitchen and living areas, placed at one end of the house, include floor-to-ceiling glass doors that lead to a deck. At the other end of the first floor are the main bedroom, ensuite and study, separated by a change in floor level. 'The floor plan is quite simple. But we wanted to ensure a level of privacy between the spaces,' says Halloran, who included a limestone fireplace between the main bedroom and living areas.

On the ground floor are three children's bedrooms, a shared bathroom, laundry and a large play area. 'There's now plenty of room for the children to play inside. But the property is still large enough to explore (approximately 1500 square metres), even with two houses on the site,' says Halloran.

Photography by Albert Comper

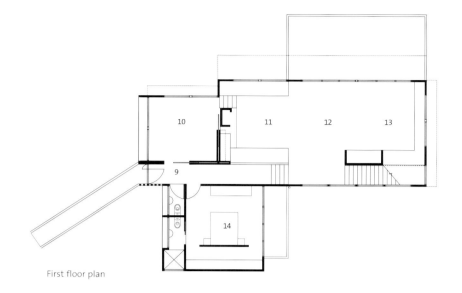

First floor plan

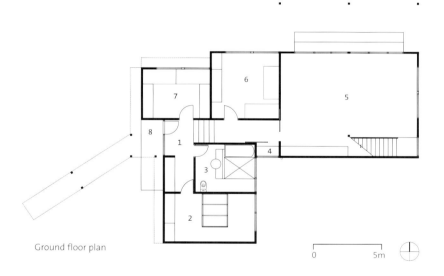

Ground floor plan

0   5m

1 Ground floor entry
2 Bedroom 2
3 Bathroom
4 Laundry
5 Play area
6 Bedroom 4
7 Bedroom 3
8 Deck
9 First floor entry
10 Study
11 Lounge
12 Dining
13 Kitchen
14 Bedroom 1

1950s Simplicity

'It's not a large house, but the idea is to use all the space.'

The owners of this house at Point Lonsdale, Victoria, didn't have to look too far to build their new beach house. 'They still own the house next door, which they lived in for years,' says architect Julian Kosloff, a director of BKK Architects. 'They still wanted to hold on to their old house, now used by the extended family when they come down,' he adds.

The brief was to design a modest beach house for a retired couple, something that required little or no maintenance. 'They definitely didn't want an ostentatious house. They were more interested in the simple 1950s-style timber homes in the area,' says Kosloff.

The house features strong elements from the 1950s. There are skillion-shaped roofs on both levels. There are also floor-to-ceiling picture windows and large sliding doors to a northern terrace. And like many of the post-war homes at Point Lonsdale, this house is entirely clad in Western red cedar. 'We also used timber on the underside of the soffit,' says Kosloff, referring to the white-painted joinery detail.

In keeping with the brief, the floor plan of the house is straightforward. The lounge and dining areas, together with a timber kitchen, are on the ground floor. A second bedroom, bathroom and laundry are a few steps above this open-plan area. The change in level not only follows the contours of the land, but also allows for a differentiation of function.

The main bedroom and ensuite are on the first level, which also features a reading area on the other side of the staircase. Like the ground floor, which has access to a terrace, the upstairs bedroom opens to a long north-facing deck. 'The quality of the light is quite special,' says Kosloff, who deliberately eliminated any corridors. 'It's not a large house, but the idea is to use all the space,' he adds.

Photography by Shannon McGrath

First floor plan

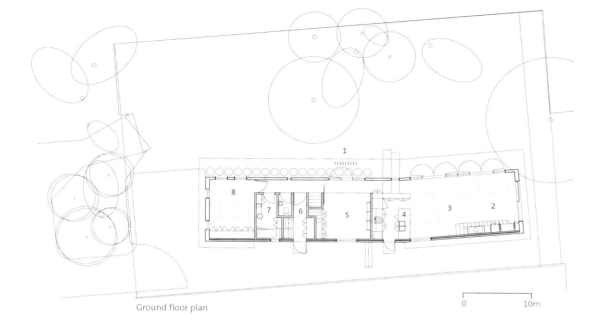

1   Entry
2   Lounge
3   Dining
4   Kitchen
5   Study
6   Laundry
7   Bathroom
8   Bedroom 1
9   Bedroom 2
10 Ensuite
11 Reading room
12 Deck

Ground floor plan

0   10m

Views of Swan Bay

JAM ARCHITECTS

'Our clients wanted the house to be hidden from the street.'

Located at Point Lonsdale, Victoria, this beach house has impressive views of Swan Bay, a shallow bay that is a sanctuary for bird life. Only 50 metres from the beach, the house takes a back seat to the vista. 'Our clients wanted the house to be hidden from the street,' says architect Chris Manton, a director of JAM Architects.

As a result, the front façade of the house is almost entirely clad in spotted gum timber battens and stone. Even the roof terrace is concealed by timber battens extending beyond the roofline. As discreet is the approach to the house. Entering along the side, one passes low-level windows and under a cantilevered first floor. 'The front room is used as a study. One of the owners wanted an outlook, but also the privacy,' says Manton.

The beach house was designed for two families, one living in Melbourne, the other in New York. 'The Melbourne contingent uses the house most weekends, while the New Yorkers tend to use it over the summer break,' says Manton, who was mindful of this aspect when designing the house.

On the ground floor, at the front of the house, is a large study that is separated from two bedrooms and two bathrooms by a double-height void (also the entrance lobby). As the

Melbourne owner uses the house more frequently, her bedroom is located on the first floor, benefiting from views over Swan Bay.

The main living areas are on the first floor. Separated from the bedroom by the void, the living areas benefit from a large northern deck. While the kitchen and living areas are open plan, the spaces are delineated by an open fireplace, clad in timber veneer, like the kitchen joinery.

To accentuate the view, as well as maximise the light, the architects included a skillion-shaped roof. Highlight glass windows below the roofline also accentuate the vista. The prized view can also be enjoyed on the roof terrace from where there are 360-degree views as far as Queenscliff.

Photography by Tony Miller

1 Lobby
2 Study
3 Bedroom
4 Bathroom
5 Laundry
6 Storage
7 Void
8 Living
9 Dining
10 Kitchen
11 Deck

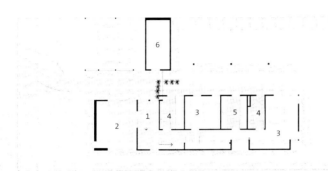

First floor plan

Ground floor plan

Timber Lantern

B A R K   D E S I G N   A R C H I T E C T S

'We wanted to keep the landscape as pristine as possible.'

At night, this house at Mt Ninderry on the Sunshine Coast hinterland looks like a timber lantern. Surrounded by native bush, the timber battens surrounding the house diffuse the internal lights. 'Our clients wanted a house that was relatively lightweight. They didn't want the house to disrupt the landscape,' says architect Stephen Guthrie, a co-director of Bark Design Architects.

Located on a steep site, the house has 180-degree views over the Pacific Ocean. With views from Noosa through to Maroochydore, the only distraction is the impressive gum trees. 'We wanted to keep the landscape as pristine as possible,' says Guthrie, noting that only one tree was removed from the 5000-square-metre property during construction.

As the house is located in a high bushfire zone, the house is fully enclosed by aluminium screens, similar to fly-wire screens. 'They were designed to prevent burning embers from entering the house,' says Guthrie, who was also mindful of using robust and lightweight materials to prevent landscape erosion. As a result, the house is made of structural steel, glass, timber battens, steel cladding and fibro cement. 'These materials are also economical,' says Guthrie, who was given a reasonably tight budget to work with.

The house is spread over several levels. One enters the house through the kitchen and living areas, before moving up a half flight of stairs to two bedrooms and a bathroom. Another half flight of stairs connects to the main bedroom suite. And views through the bush are available throughout the house. The main bedroom, for example, overlooks the living area on one side and the outdoor living area on the other. To ensure privacy, this bedroom features louvres on either side, which can be closed for privacy, but also partially or fully opened for cross-ventilation.

One of the most pleasurable aspects of this beach house is the number of outdoor decks, five in total. There's even a deck used for drying clothes during the warmer months. 'The house is designed over several levels. But because they're only half levels, the rooms appear to merge with each other,' says Guthrie.

Photography by David Sandison

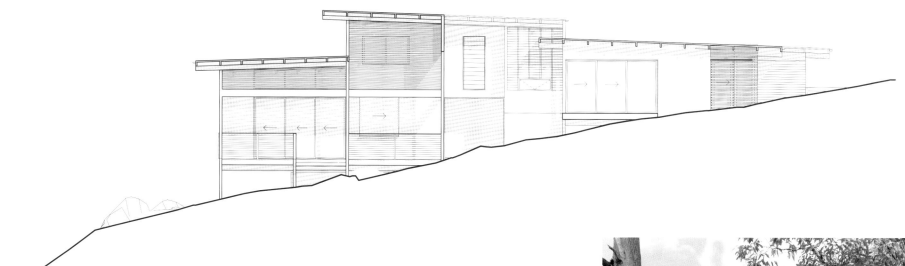

North elevation

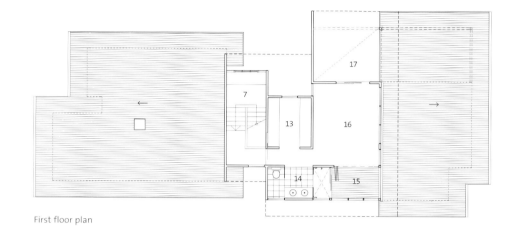

First floor plan

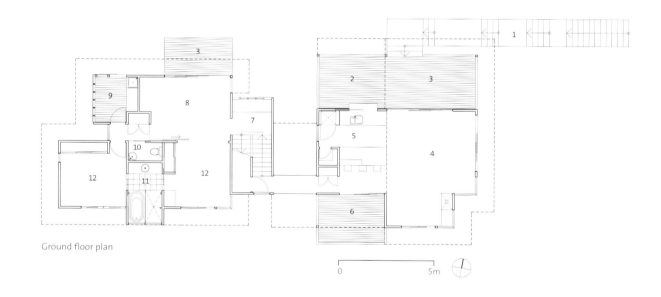

Ground floor plan

0 _____ 5m

1 Entry steps	10 Powder room
2 Outdoor dining	11 Bathroom
3 Outdoor living	12 Bedroom
4 Living/dining	13 Walk-in robe
5 Kitchen	14 Ensuite
6 Southern deck	15 Bedroom deck
7 Stairway	16 Main bedroom
8 Lounge	17 Void below
9 Laundry/drying deck	

Amid the Moonahs

'You feel as though you're swimming into the moonah trees.'

Located at Sorrento, on Victoria's Mornington Peninsula, this two-storey beach house is spread across a few levels. 'The levels follow the contours of the sand dunes,' says architect Richard Kerr.

Designed for a couple with three adult children, the house was conceived as a more permanent abode. 'They wanted a relaxed beach house, but they also wanted something that was comfortable and enduring,' says Kerr. The owners had seen a house at Yea in Victoria, also designed by Kerr. 'They wanted the same materials for their house,' says Kerr, referring to the West Australian limestone and grey ironbark. In addition to these materials, recycled timber piers (once in a wharf in Sydney) frame the entrance. 'The materials recall Frank Lloyd Wright,' says Kerr, referring to the stone plinth in the Sorrento house.

The limestone and timber house is long and narrow and follows the dimensions of the property (24 metres wide by 83 metres long). On the ground floor are three bedrooms, a bathroom and powder room together with the entry lobby. A few steps above the lobby, on the other side of the bedroom wing, is a second living area, used also as a media room.

On the first floor, on the lower side, are the main bedroom, dressing area and ensuite, together with a study. This level also includes the open-plan dining and kitchen area. And on the higher side, elevated five steps above the kitchen and dining areas, is the main living area, which leads to a large deck.

The main living and dining areas also have a Wrightian feel, with a raked timber ceiling in the lounge and a built-in window seat in the dining area. Limestone flooring in both spaces adds to the slightly earthy texture in the home. 'It seemed appropriate to place the main living spaces on the first floor. That's where the views are,' says Kerr, who appreciates the view from the deck. 'From here, you look above the moonahs as well as under the canopy,' he says.

One of the other best vantage points is from the swimming pool, half of which features an infinity edge. The pool projects over the dunes, where the land falls away. 'You feel as though you're swimming into the moonah trees,' says Kerr.

Photography by Derek Swalwell

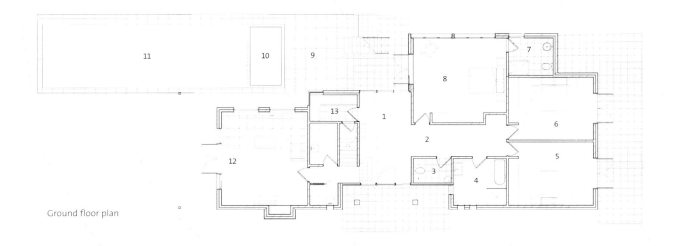

Ground floor plan

First floor plan

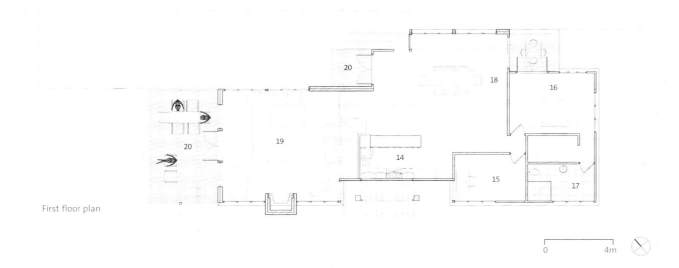

1   Entry
2   Hall
3   Powder room
4   Bathroom
5   Bedroom 4
6   Bedroom 3
7   Ensuite
8   Bedroom 2
9   Pool terrace
10 Spa
11 Pool
12 Living
13 Laundry
14 Kitchen
15 Study
16 Bedroom 1
17 Ensuite
18 Dining
19 Main living
20 Deck

0   4m

Prefab Views

BURO ARCHITECTURE + INTERIORS

'It's a relatively compact house. But it has everything you need.'

Sandy Point, a two-and-a-half-hour drive from Melbourne, is a comfortable distance for those seeking to get away. The owners, a couple with children, fell in love with a vacant site. 'They realised they could take in views to the beach if they built a two-storey house,' says architect Stephen Javens, a director of BURO Architecture + Interiors.

Because the clients paid more for the vacant site than they originally expected to, they had to reduce the original budget to build the house. The most economical solution was to have the beach house prefabricated. 'We found a factory in Bendigo that used to construct the portable school rooms we all had in the 1960s and 70s. They were able to produce our design,' says Javens. As the market for portable classrooms has declined, the owners of the factory were more than happy to build a house.

Designed in three sections to allow the house to be transported by three trucks, the house was almost fully complete before it left the factory. 'Once it arrived, we only had to bolt it together and add some plaster board to conceal the joins,' says Javens. 'Even the light bulbs were in place,' he adds. The site had been prepared with 16 holes made for the footings of the house.

The steel-framed house is clad with timber and has a steel roof. On the ground floor are two bedrooms, a bathroom, a laundry and storeroom. And on the first floor are the kitchen, living and dining areas, leading to a large deck. The main bedroom, ensuite and powder room are behind the kitchen. 'It's a relatively compact house (approximately 220 square metres). But it has everything you need,' says Javens, who sees little point in adding marble bench tops to a casual beach house. 'Our clients can add to the finishes down the track. But that's not what brings them down here,' he adds, pointing out the beach views.

Photography by David Trewern

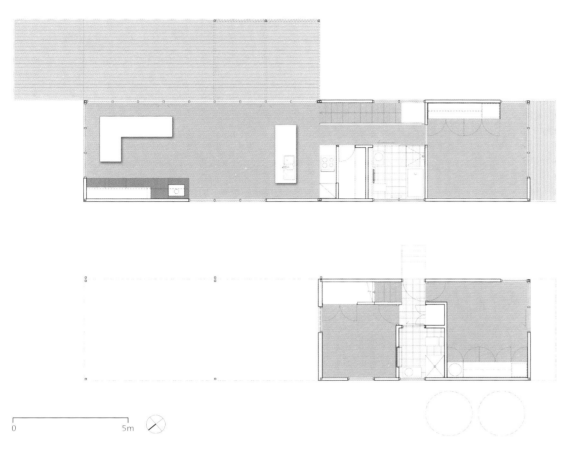

0   5m

The Sands

R O B E R T   A N D A R Y   A R C H I T E C T U R E

'It's quite magical at night, seeing the reflections.'

Adjacent to an 18-hole golf course, 'The Sands' at Torquay was conceived as an architectural enclave. Designed for permanent residents, as well as for weekenders, the relative proximity to Melbourne (just over an hour's drive) allows for flexible use.

This house is one of the first seen upon entering the estate. A few blocks down from the clubhouse and the soon-to-be-completed hotel, it can't be missed. Spread over three levels, the house has views of the 18th hole and sand dunes in the distance.

The house is constructed in steel and timber frame with compressed cement cladding and plywood. 'The client's son is a carpenter by trade. I designed the house so he could easily strap up with a tool kit and build it,' says architect Robert Andary.

The three-level home includes a two car-garage, enclosed by cedar doors. A large gallery entry space with a double-height void is on the ground level. There are also two bedrooms, a bathroom and laundry, together with a sitting room that overlooks a pond. This pond partially frames the ground floor. 'It's quite magical at night, seeing the reflections,' says Andary.

The middle level comprises open-plan living areas. At one end of the floorplate is the living area, with views towards the water. On the opposite side is the dining area, together with a second, more formal, living area. Separating these two living areas is the kitchen, with a slot-like window overlooking the clubhouse. The third level comprises the main bedroom, ensuite and walk-in dressing areas, with the bedroom benefiting from an adjoining terrace.

Andary deliberately used sombre tones for this beach house. Dark, moody rendered walls in rainforest blacks and brownish hues feature on the exterior. 'There was a council policy down here restricting the use of light-reflective colours. The palette had to recede into the landscape,' says Andary. One of the other distinctive features of the house is its skewed middle level. 'I wanted to create a dynamic form. But I also wanted to open the house to these views, while reducing the impact to the street,' he adds.

Photography by James Kreltszheim

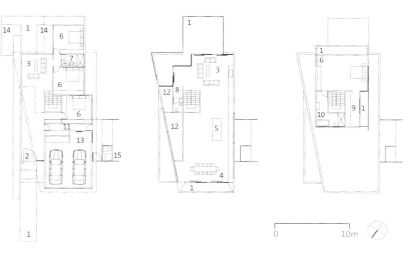

1	Deck	6	Bedroom	11	Laundry
2	Entry	7	Bathroom	12	Void
3	Living	8	Powder room	13	Garage
4	Dining	9	Walk-in robe	14	Pond
5	Kitchen	10	Ensuite	15	Store

In Context

SWANEY DRAPER ARCHITECTS

'The dining area is pivotal to the design. It brings the family together.'

This property at Barwon Heads, Victoria, had been in the same family for years. Only half an hour past Geelong, it's surrounded by rolling sand dunes and a golf course. With Bass Strait providing the backdrop, the property feels considerably more isolated than it actually is. Perched on a hill, the beach house enjoys panoramic views to the hinterlands.

The design brief included respecting the 1920s clubhouse on the adjacent golf course. 'They didn't want to recreate the 1920s building. It was a case of acknowledging its existence,' says architect Simon Swaney, who worked closely with architect Sally Draper. 'There's quite a lot of family history associated with the property. The owner didn't want a beach house that looked as though it had just been erected in days,' adds Swaney.

Drawing upon the local moonah trees as well as the clubhouse, the architects used materials that suggested context. Rammed earth walls, drawn from a local quarry, form the basis for one of the pavilions in the home. The other pavilions feature grey weathered timbers. And all the pavilions feature pitched roofs, like the 1920s clubhouse.

The house comprises one long two-storey pavilion and a smaller pavilion. The large pavilion contains the main bedroom on the first floor, and the kitchen, service area and an area for bunk beds on the ground floor. 'It's quite a solid pavilion. It's south-facing and receives the harshest winds,' says Swaney. In contrast, the other pavilions face north and are considerably lighter in feel. These single-storey pavilions contain the living areas, one formal, the other informal. Bridging the two living spaces is the dining area, leading to a large timber deck.

In contrast to the living spaces, with pitched roofs and limed timber trusses, the dining area features a flat ceiling. 'The dining area is pivotal to the design. It brings the family together. It also connects the views of the water to the golf green,' says Swaney, who framed views in some of the more exposed spaces. The long slot-style window in the formal living area allows privacy, while still maintaining views to the head of the river. 'It's quite an exposed site. But from inside, the views belong entirely to the owners,' he adds.

138

Photography by Trevor Mein

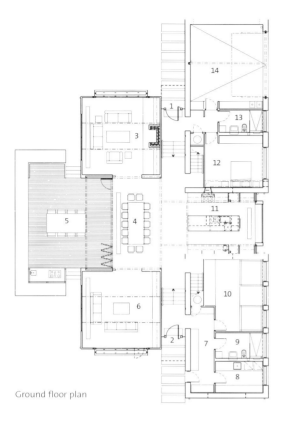

Ground floor plan

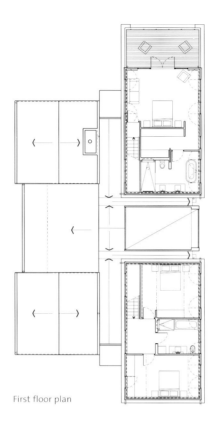

First floor plan

1 Entry 1
2 Entry 2
3 Living 1
4 Dining
5 Deck 1
6 Living 2
7 Sand room
8 Laundry
9 Bathroom 2
10 Bunk room
11 Kitchen
12 Guest
13 Bathroom
14 Garage

Designed to Last

SWANEY DRAPER ARCHITECTS

'This house is a retreat, not a city home.'

The sound of surf fills this house at Lorne, overlooking Victoria's Great Ocean Road. The crashing waves literally appear to be at the doorstep. 'Our clients had been looking for a site to build on for some time. They wanted to be slightly outside the township, and a little more isolated,' says architect Simon Swaney, who designed this house with architect Sally Draper.

The architects excavated 4 metres on the relatively steep site to nestle the house between neighbours. And to ensure privacy from the winding coastal road, a 3-metre cantilevered deck was added. 'Our clients didn't want to feel like goldfish in a bowl. This house is a retreat, not a city home,' says Swaney.

The brief was to create a large home that took advantage of the vista over Loutitt Bay. While the outlook from the lighthouse at Airey's Inlet to the pier at Lorne is impressive, so is the wind chill, particularly during the winter months. 'We knew we had to create a more temperate environment,' says Swaney, who created a protected rear courtyard as well as front decks. However, the architects were also mindful of not sacrificing water views for comfort. As a result, there are unimpeded views from the rear terrace and lawn through glass doors on either side of the living areas.

The house, clad in black-stained timber, features a striking 8-metre-high sandstone spine wall. Slicing the house into two, this wall also delineates bedrooms from living areas. Containing two fireplaces and areas for wood storage, the sandstone wall and hearth extend from the front deck and lounge to the rear courtyard. 'The idea was to blur the indoors with the outdoors,' says Swaney.

The kitchen is placed to one side of the living area. The central island bench, made of stone, includes two sinks and occupies a premier position. The dining area features a cantilevered built-in window box. Externally framed by an aluminium 'picture frame', the seat with its large picture window is one of the most favoured spots in the house. Louvred blinds, operated automatically, ensure the amount of sunlight is controlled.

Spaces are carefully arranged over six levels. The children's play area, leading from the kitchen, is oriented to the north and rear courtyard. Featuring glass bi-fold doors, this room opens to a small patch of lawn. In contrast, the main bedroom occupies the top level of the house. Designed like a retreat, it features a built-in study at one end and an open-plan bathroom at the other.

This beach house has a timeless quality. 'It's not just about natural ventilation and using recycled materials. It's as important to design a building that lasts,' says Swaney.

Photography by Trevor Mein

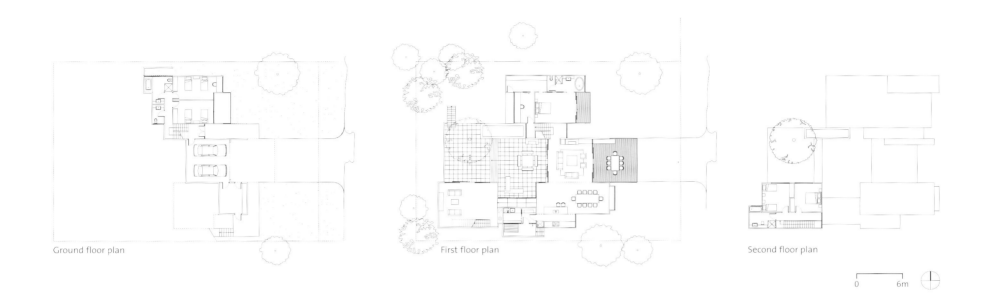

Ground floor plan

First floor plan

Second floor plan

0   6m

Lang Cove

'We wanted to ensure the house could be adjusted to suit the prevailing winds or sunlight.'

This region of Northland, New Zealand, is predominantly farmland. However, the area is also known for its beaches, many of which, like Lang Cove, are relatively protected from the elements. Only an hour-and-a-half drive from Auckland, on the east coast of the North Island, Lang Cove is a popular destination for weekenders.

This house, located at the southern end of the beach, is only separated from the sand by a 50-metre-wide grassed reserve. Like most popular beach resorts, there are houses either side. 'Our clients wanted privacy from neighbours. They wanted to feel as though they were on their own, at least when they're inside the house,' says architect Jason Bailey, director of Bailey Architects. Privacy was achieved by using carefully positioned fin walls to maintain lateral screening without blocking the views.

The original timber home on the site was mostly demolished. Walls from the original garage, together with a small amount of structure surrounding the entrance were incorporated in the new building. The new two-storey house is a combination of materials: painted pine weatherboard combined with in situ concrete for walls, plus glass and aluminium. Aluminium louvred screens form an important component

of the design. 'It's quite a calm environment, but the site is fairly exposed. We wanted to ensure the house could be adjusted in response to the prevailing winds or sunlight,' says Bailey, drawing across one of the external aluminium louvred screens on the terrace.

As the house is at the end of a relatively steep drive, one steps down from the garage into the main living area on the ground floor. The ground floor also includes a kitchen to one side of the living areas, a bedroom and separate office, as well as a laundry and powder room. The main bedroom, on the first floor, has a large sitting area, as well as a large terrace. The mezzanine-style bedroom also benefits from views over the lounge and across to the beach. 'The house was designed for a couple with adult children. They often come here on their own,' says Bailey, who didn't want the house to feel over-scaled. 'The upstairs is almost self-contained,' he adds.

Photography by Kallan MacLeod

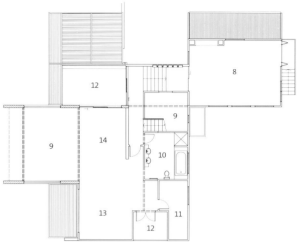

Upper level floor plan

Lower level floor plan

1   Garage
2   Laundry
3   Bathroom
4   Office
5   Bedroom 2
6   Lounge
7   Sitting
8   Guest bedroom
9   Void
10 Bathroom
11 Walk-in robe
12 Balcony
13 Master bedroom sitting
14 Master bedroom

Zigzagging Along the Coast

C A S E Y   B R O W N   A R C H I T E C T U R E

'It just seemed the right place to build a weekender.'

This beach house at Stanwell Park, New South Wales, appears to zigzag along the coast. 'It was designed to capture views from every vantage point,' says architect Rob Brown, co-director of Casey Brown Architecture. 'The concept came from the office, where everyone wants the best view at work. But most end up compromising,' says Brown, who wasn't prepared to do so for this beach house.

Located an hour's drive south of Sydney, Stanwell Park is one of a handful of coal-mining towns on this escarpment. 'The region's claim to fame is that DH Lawrence wrote his novel *Kangaroo* here,' says Brown. For the owners, a couple with children, the place offered childhood memories. 'One of the owners spent holidays here. It just seemed the right place to build a weekender,' he adds.

Originally a 1950s fibro shack stood on the property, only metres from the surf beach. With a richly planted escarpment behind and ocean views ahead, the site offered the perfect northeast aspect. 'Our clients owned the shack for years. But it had deteriorated,' says Brown, recalling the termites and rot.

The new multi-level house is made of concrete, steel, local basalt and timber. In contrast to the stone lower levels, the upper levels are built in timber and glass, creating a lighter effect. Split over four levels, the top level includes the kitchen and living area. The dining area is a few steps below, opening onto a large covered terrace with barbeque. The main bedroom and ensuite are a full level below. A guest bedroom, laundry and car parking are on the lowest level. As the house is stepped across the site, there are two ways of entering, one directly from the carport, the other via a ramp to the front door.

Unlike most houses, there are few internal walls. Each room is defined by a change in level rather than by a doorway. 'The spaces are quite independent,' says Brown. As unique is the copper skillion roof. 'In this environment, it's the material of choice. It's maintenance free and has a wonderful patina with age,' he adds.

Photography by Michael Nicholson

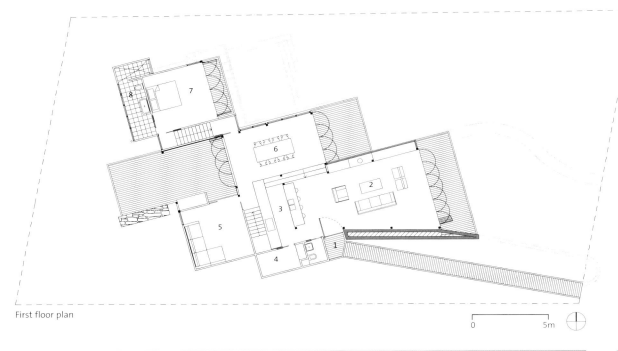

First floor plan

0   5m

1   Entry
2   Living
3   Kitchen
4   Pantry
5   Lounge
6   Dining
7   Master bedroom
8   Master ensuite

A Great Opportunity

S J B   A R C H I T E C T S

'Copper was an ideal material ...
it always has a wonderful patina.'

This property at St Andrews Beach, Victoria, was vacant for a considerable time. While the tea-treed site, set in the dunes, was only a short distance from the surf beach, it was unusually steep, falling approximately 13 metres from the road. Height control limits set by the local council also deterred prospective purchasers.

However, for the owners, a couple with young children, the property excited them from first inspection. 'I tried to share their excitement. But I was cautious about the challenges ahead,' says architect Alfred de Bruyne, a director of SJB Architects.

While de Bruyne was looking at ways to build a beach house, the owners were talking romantically about the classic Aussie beach house: restrained, honest, simple and easy to live in. 'They wanted the children to be able to return to the house with sand between their toes, not worrying about bringing it into the house,' says de Bruyne.

From the street, the house appears as a single storey. Clad in copper, it is closed to the street. 'Copper was an ideal material. It stands up to the salt air. It always has a wonderful patina,' says de Bruyne, who included large timber sleepers in the forecourt to create a similar rustic feel.

Past the glass-and-timber door, the house opens up to the view. The top level, also the point of access, includes a separate family room at the front of the house. This room, used by the children, is separated from the open-plan kitchen, dining and living area by an internal courtyard. 'We wanted to get northern light into the house. But we also wanted to create separation between the two living areas,' says de Bruyne. A large terrace, accessed via stackable glass doors, extends the indoor space.

A staircase adjacent to the kitchen leads to the lower level: a main bedroom, ensuite, a study, three bedrooms and a bathroom, accessed both externally and internally. 'The owners aren't precious about the house. But if the children return from the beach covered in sand, they don't have to drag it through the house,' says de Bruyne.

While the house appears moody from the street, the interior is light and transparent. Highlight clerestory windows hover above the kitchen, and the living area is framed by glass on three sides. And although the house appears relatively modest in scale from the street, it is in reality a large family weekender. 'The children love it. There's a play area in the backyard. But as the land falls away, there are also pockets below the house for the children to explore'.

Photography by Tony Miller

Lower ground floor plan

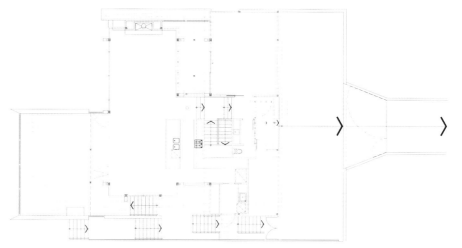

Ground floor plan

Designed from Afar

D A N I E L   M A R S H A L L   A R C H I T E C T

'We wanted the owners to be able to look though the living areas to the sea.'

The architect of this house in New Zealand didn't meet the owners until the house was being constructed. At the time, the owners were living in the United Kingdom, planning a return to New Zealand to live permanently. The design evolved by phone and the internet. The final stages relied on a DVD (an animated film) together with a physical model of the house, shipped over to the UK.

The initial brief for the house at Omaha (an hour's drive north of Auckland), was Cape Cod style. 'It wasn't a style our office is known for. We prefer creating contemporary homes,' says architect Daniel Marshall. As a way of finding a compatible path, Marshall suggested the owners look at a book on the architecture of the Hamptons (Long Island, New York). 'Many of these homes are quite contemporary,' he adds.

The site, perched above the beach, was also influential in the design. Because it is relatively exposed to the southeast winds, the architects felt a protected courtyard space was required. As a result, the cedar-clad and glass house features a courtyard garden, protected from the wind by a single-storey living pavilion. 'We wanted the owners to be able to look though the living areas to the sea, rather than feeling closed off,' says Marshall.

On the ground floor are the kitchen, dining and living areas, together with a second raised sitting area. The two living areas are separated by American oak joinery, one side functioning as storage, while the other side (sitting area) includes an open fireplace. At the front of the house, facing the street, are three bedrooms and a bathroom. 'You can see the water from wherever you are in the house,' says Marshall, pointing out the vista from one of the bedrooms.

On the first floor are the main bedroom and ensuite, together with a dressing area. There is also a separate bunkroom. Marshall included a balcony, accessed via the main bedroom, to allow the sea views to be enjoyed at all times. 'It's a reasonably transparent house. The coastal dunes are integral to the design,' says Marshall, who included glass sliding doors in most rooms.

While the house isn't Cape Cod style, there are finely sculptured nooks within the essentially rectilinear form. The cedar plywood ceiling in the sitting area is faceted. And three smaller canopies protruding over the deck have a fine sense of craftsmanship. 'It is contemporary, but it's not just a minimal glass box,' says Marshall.

Photography by Daniel Marshall

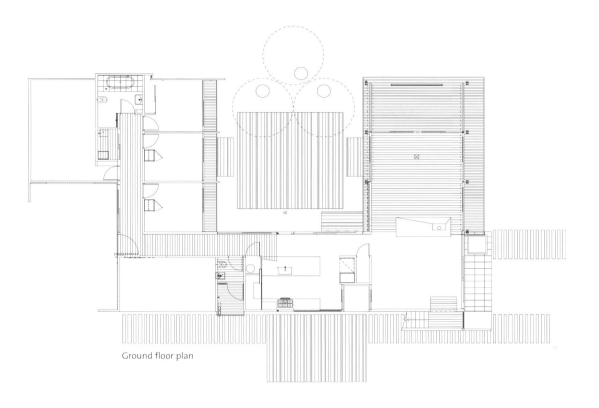

Ground floor plan

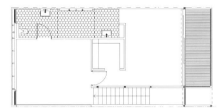

First floor plan

The Colour of Tea-trees

MARCUS O'REILLY ARCHITECTS

'I wanted to use robust materials, ones that would improve with age.'

Located at Sorrento, on Victoria's Mornington Peninsula, this beach house picks up the colours of the surrounding tea-trees. The cedar-clad house has been stained green and many of the timbers used are bleached grey. 'The materials capture some of the earlier homes built in the area,' says architect Marcus O'Reilly, pointing out the tea-tree stakes used to screen the sun and the home's sandstone base.

Positioned on the side of a sand dune, the dominant outlook is over a heavily treed site. Limestone outcrops appear on the 1300-square-metre site, which overlooks a nature reserve, creating a buffer to a neighbouring property. 'It's quite private here. We're abutting a national park,' says O'Reilly.

While the owners didn't have a clear image in their minds at the start of the design process, they were extremely familiar with the area. 'The property has been in the family for the last 50 years. Originally there was a 90-square-metre shack. Eventually, it became too small,' says O'Reilly.

The house was designed to accommodate a couple with three teenage children, as well as extended family and pets. The brief included distinct zones for the children and their friends. 'The idea was the children could play billiards or table tennis without disturbing the entire family,' says O'Reilly. 'They also wanted something that was low maintenance,' he adds.

Behind the stone podium is a place for the owner's boat, a table-tennis table, parking for two cars and a storeroom. Access to the house is via wide timber treads with galvanised steel plate balustrades. 'I wanted to use robust materials, ones that would improve with age,' says O'Reilly.

Like most informal beach houses, the entrance leads straight into the open-plan living areas, with a kitchen at one end, and a living area at the other. The raked timber ceiling and polished floorboards produce an informal ambience. While meals are eaten inside, they are also served up on the large timber terrace, complete with barbeque. To ensure the deck could also be used in cooler months, a polycarbonate and timber awning was included. 'Even in winter you get the wonderful northern sun,' O'Reilly adds.

In keeping with the owner's request for distance between children and adults, the parents' bedroom wing is placed to one side of the living areas, while the children's bedrooms, together with a separate rumpus room, are on the other. 'There's a slight boomerang shape in the design,' says O'Reilly. 'The shape responds to the dunes,' he adds.

Photography by Dianna Snape and Marcus O'Reilly

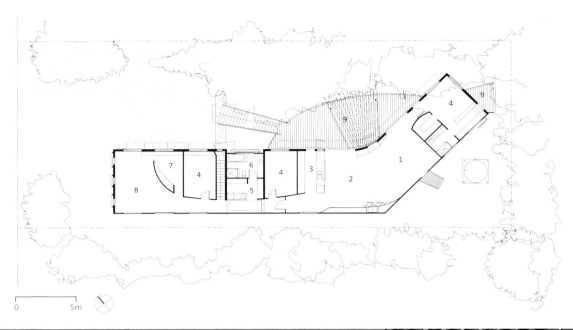

1 Lounge
2 Dining
3 Kitchen
4 Bedroom
5 Laundry
6 Bathroom
7 Study
8 Sunroom
9 Deck

Blue Sky and Ocean

ODDEN RODRIGUES ARCHITECTS

'I didn't want the house to compete with this view.'

This house is only an hour's drive south of Perth's CBD. 'The area will soon be an outer suburb,' says architect Simon Rodrigues. Overlooking Avalon Point and with views to the Indian Ocean, the house is slightly oriented to the northwest. 'You get the winter sun as well as unimpeded views directly ahead,' he adds.

While the house is on the fringe of town, it still enjoys unspoilt coastal heath and dune vegetation. 'It's relatively low-lying and often quite windy,' says Rodrigues. The brief to the architects was for a simple and sturdy house for a couple with three young children. 'One of the owners spent summer holidays in the area. They wanted something quite robust, like many of the homes built in the 1960s and 70s. They didn't want a townhouse on the coast,' he adds.

While it isn't made of fibro cement and perched on stilts like homes of that period, the house is relatively simple, both in form and materials used. Made from concrete tilt panels, galvanised steel beams, concrete floors and a steel roof, the house extends over three levels. Part of the ground floor is nestled into the sand dunes, with half this level almost submerged. This bunker-like area includes storage for rubber dinghies, fishing gear, a pool table and car parking. Craypots and an endless number of surfboards are also housed in this area.

The first level, oriented to the beach, contains five bedrooms, including the main bedroom that leads to a terrace. To maximise views, the living areas are on the top level. The open-plan kitchen, living and dining area includes dramatic picture windows. Divided by a viewing platform that's accessed by a ladder, the vista includes a rich palette of blues, from the ocean to the sky.

This beach house has a strong industrial aesthetic. Floors are concrete, as are many of the walls. And some of the doors are made of steel. 'The owners found many of the fittings in second-hand yards,' says Rodrigues, pointing out the stainless steel basins in the bathrooms. Some of the artifacts, such as the art in the living area, once appeared behind a hotel bar in Perth. 'The house is really quite restrained. I didn't want the house to compete with this view. It's essentially the blue sky and the ocean,' says Rodrigues modestly.

Photography by Robert Frith

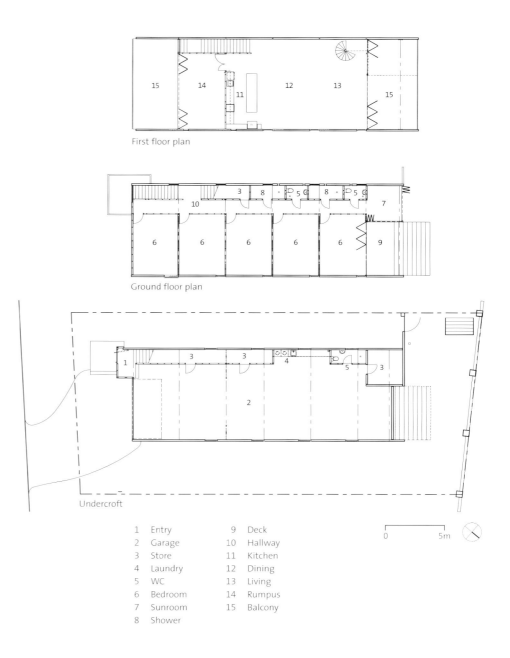

First floor plan

Ground floor plan

Undercroft

1	Entry	9	Deck
2	Garage	10	Hallway
3	Store	11	Kitchen
4	Laundry	12	Dining
5	WC	13	Living
6	Bedroom	14	Rumpus
7	Sunroom	15	Balcony
8	Shower		

0   5m

Reaching for the Sun

STRACHAN GROUP ARCHITECTS

'The breezeway is the core of the design.'

This beach house is nestled among kanuka trees at Mangawhai Heads, a one-and-a-half-hour drive north of Auckland. The site, on the southern slope of the sand dunes, is a short walk from an estuary. The surrounds feel unusually lightweight for the New Zealand landscape. 'The owners spent time on Victoria's Mornington Peninsula. The bush landscape at Northland is similarly soft and feathery,' says architect David Strachan, a director of Strachan Group Architects (SGA).

Designed for a large and extended family, the initial concept for the beach house was a series of cottages or pods in the bush. 'The owners were keen to retain as many of the trees as possible. When the area of all the pods was combined, the footprint became considerable,' says Strachan, who was asked to include six bedrooms in the design.

Rather than create a series of pods connected by covered walkways, SGA designed one long and narrow two-storey building. Approximately 5 metres wide (the width of one room) and 35 metres long, the dimensions allowed most of the trees on the site to be saved.

From the street, the cedar and timber-battened house appears relatively closed. Oriented to the south, the front façade features small openings, both windows and doors. 'It gets quite cold here. The southern winds are memorable,' says Strachan. In contrast to the closed front façade,

the rear, northern façade is almost fully glazed. The angled roofline reaches towards the sun to maximise the amount of sunlight entering the home during the colder months.

The living areas, along with most of the bedrooms, are located on the first floor. Four bedrooms, including the main bedroom and ensuite, are located to one side of a breezeway or outdoor room, while the kitchen, dining and living areas are located to the other side. Like a suitcase, the breezeway can be opened up to a northern deck by means of a garage-like tilt door, as well as to the south, via insulating timber sliding shutters. 'The breezeway is the core of the design. It's used for alfresco dining, or simply as a second, more casual living area,' says Strachan, who used the same timber batten detailing on the interior walls of the breezeway.

As the house is on the southern side of a sand dune, getting light into the house proved one of the most challenging aspects. 'We could have removed a few of the trees. But they're integral to the experience of being here,' says Strachan.

Photography by Patrick Reynolds

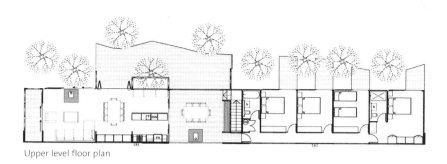

Upper level floor plan

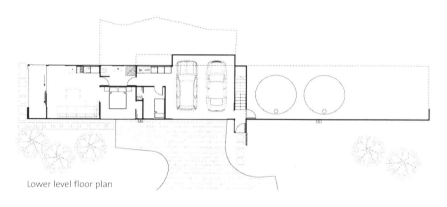

Lower level floor plan

A Growing Family

B E R N A R D   S E E B E R   A R C H I T E C T S

'It's important to connect to a neighbourhood.'

This beach house in Western Australia was originally a brick Californian bungalow. The relatively modest home accommodated a family of five. 'When the owners found they were expecting twins, they knew more room was required,' says architect Bernard Seeber.

Instead of demolishing the bungalow, Seeber refurbished the house to include four children's bedrooms together with a separate play area at the front of the cottage, once a verandah. Seeber also removed a lean-to. 'It was probably the coldest part of the house. It was south-facing and damp,' he says.

The cottage was simply rendered and painted white. A new steel roof was added, also painted white. 'We wanted to keep the streetscape intact,' says Seeber. However, to cater for the family's growing needs, a substantial contemporary wing was added to the rear of the bungalow. Clad in Colorbond and also painted white, the two-storey wing is a sharp contrast to the more enclosed bungalow. 'Our clients wished to maintain the relaxed lifestyle once common in the locality, with an open house and outdoor recreation space,' says Seeber, signaling the beach a few hundred metres away.

The ground floor of the new wing is one large open space. The kitchen is at one end; the living area at the other. To take advantage of the sea breezes, stackable glass doors allow the living areas to open up completely to the garden. In contrast, the main bedroom, ensuite, study and large music room on the first floor are more enclosed. The windows are protected by a mesh blind, which not only screens the glare, but still allows light to permeate the living areas during the cooler months.

From the street, the house appears modest in scale. However, the scale of the new wing can be fully appreciated from a side street, leading to the beach. 'It's fairly open (to the side street). It's important to connect to a neighbourhood,' says Seeber.

Photography by Robert Frith

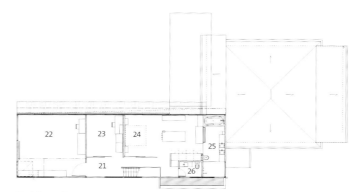

First floor plan

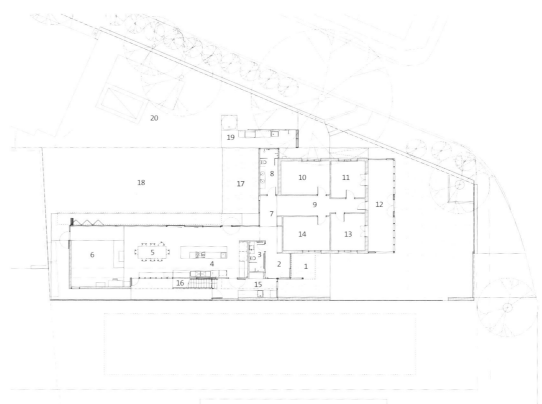

Ground floor plan

1	Deck landing	10	Bedroom 2	19	BBQ
2	Entry	11	Bedroom 3	20	Playground
3	Bathroom 3	12	Play den	21	Stair landing
4	Kitchen	13	Bedroom 4	22	Music room and lounge
5	Dining	14	Bedroom 5	23	Study and guest room
6	Living	15	Laundry	24	Bedroom 1
7	North entry	16	Stair	25	Bathroom 1
8	Bathroom 2	17	North deck	26	WC
9	Bungalow hall	18	North lawn		

On a Ridge

'It's a great place for alfresco dining or simply just looking out to the ocean.'

This house is located in the Cape Region of Western Australia. Approximately 270 kilometres south of Perth, the house looks towards the Indian Ocean on one side and Geographe Bay on the other. 'It was previously used for farming. The area was overgrazed and some of the topsoil has blown away over the years,' says architect Michael Sorensen.

The 7-hectare property has few neighbours. With strict council guidelines, including height restrictions (a maximimum of 5 metres), those seeking large double-storey homes stay away. 'The landscape is slowly regenerating. I was mindful of the grass trees and unique landscape when designing this house,' says Sorensen, who was not deterred by the height limit.

Built for a family, the house was designed to be used every weekend or two. 'The owners wanted to be able to open the door, quickly unpack and relax. They didn't want to have a list of tasks to attend to,' says Sorensen, who has extensive local knowledge and a practice at Margaret River, 30 kilometres south of the site.

The single-storey rendered brick house is painted a green-grey colour, in keeping with hues in the landscape. As the northwest and southwest winds are strong, the house includes curved roofs as well as protected courtyards. 'The roofs deflect the wind,' says Sorensen, who also incorporated two courtyards, a large half-walled summer courtyard and a high brick-walled winter retreat in the design.

While the house appears relatively modest in the landscape, it is reasonably spacious, approximately 350 square metres. Following a staggered H-plan, the kitchen, dining and living areas occupy the northern tip of the H, as does the children's rumpus room. A service pod, including the bathrooms and garage, forms the cross of the H, with the main and children's bedrooms located on the southern portion.

Although there are some coastal views from the living areas, the premier aspect is found on three rooftop decks. The central deck is covered by a roof. 'It's a great place for alfresco dining or simply just looking out to the ocean,' says Sorensen.

Photography by Olivier Marill

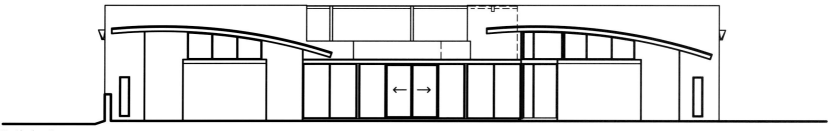

North elevation

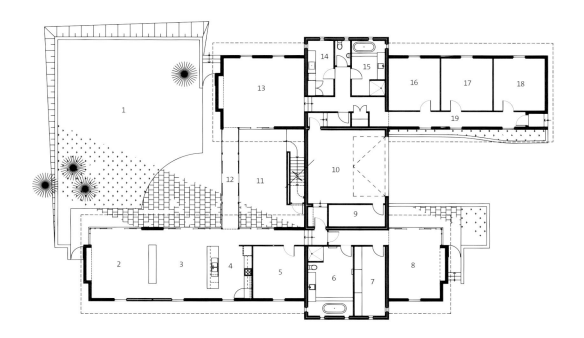

1 Courtyard
2 Living
3 Dining
4 Kitchen
5 Office
6 Bathroom 1
7 Robe
8 Bedroom 1
9 Store
10 Garage
11 Winter courtyard
12 Walkway
13 Children's room
14 Laundry
15 Bathroom 2
16 Bedroom 2
17 Bedroom 3
18 Bedroom 4
19 Hall

Pacific Views

'It's quite deceptive. It's a relatively compact house.'

This house at Tairua Beach, New Zealand, is a one-and-a-half-hour drive southeast of Auckland. Unlike many other parts of the country, which are heavily forested, this region features numerous species of cacti. 'In some ways, it feels like some of the beach resorts outside Los Angeles,' says designer Scott Fowler, director of Architektur.

The house was designed for Morgan Cronin, owner of Cronin Kitchens, who was responsible for the award-winning kitchen. 'I really can't take any credit for the kitchen. That was completely Morgan's design,' says Fowler.

The house, with floor-to-ceiling glass walls and windows, is partially enclosed by cedar battens. The front of the house faces the street and the Pacific Ocean, and features pivoting timber batten screens to increase privacy. To the rear, the façade is exposed, allowing views of an estuary.

The two elevations are quite different. From the street, the house reads as a two-storey building, with its zinc-clad walls and garage door. However, from the rear, as a result of the slope of the land, the house appears as a single storey. 'It's quite deceptive. It's a relatively compact house,' says Fowler.

The ground level comprises a double garage and circular staircase that leads to the living areas. The plan on the first floor is fairly open, with the kitchen, living and dining areas enjoying unimpeded views from the ocean to the estuary. On the other side of the house are three bedrooms, including the main, with an ensuite and walk-in dressing area.

Like many homes of the early 1960s, there's a certain informality in the arrangement of the outdoor spaces. A timber deck encircles the house and at the rear are two further timber decks, linked by a bridge or walkway. And to ensure the outdoors are used during the cooler months, an outdoor fireplace appears on the lower of the two decks, also clad with cedar battens.

Photography by Kallan MacLeod

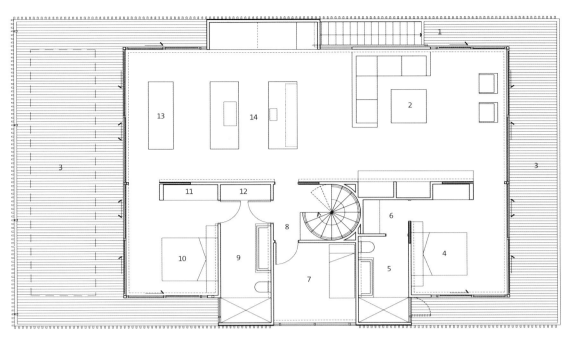

1 Entry	8 Hall
2 Living	9 Bathroom
3 Deck	10 Bedroom 2
4 Bedroom 1	11 Robe
5 Ensuite	12 Laundry
6 Robe	13 Dining
7 Bedroom 3	14 Kitchen

Designed for Two or Four

CENTRUM ARCHITECTS

'The angles were a response to the angled branches of the trees. They're quite dramatic.'

This beach house at Lorne, Victoria, was designed for a couple with adult children. 'Our brief was to design a house that would work for the whole family or just for two people,' says architect Ken Charles, who worked closely with fellow Centrum Architects directors Geoff Lavender and Alan Cubbon.

Overlooking Loutitt Bay, the site is as much about the shoreline as the hilly bush setting, dominated by established eucalypts. As the slope of the site is approximately 30 degrees, the materials used are fairly lightweight: timber and steel frames clad in Ecoply and solid timber straps. Painted a purple-red hue, the Ecoply evokes the colour of a sunset at Lorne.

Because of the steep slope, almost two-thirds of the land couldn't be built on. However, to maximise the building envelope, the house is spread over three levels. The top level, also the street level, includes a 'platform' for the parking of two cars, a study and entry vestibule. One of the most distinctive features upon arrival is the sculptural staircase made of timber, glass, painted board and steel rods. Like the angular posts at the top of the staircase, the timber feature wall is also angled. 'The angles were a response to the angled branches of the trees. They're quite dramatic,' says Charles, who placed a slot window at the top of the staircase and generous glazing below. 'We saw the staircase like a shaft of light coming from the hilltops,' he adds.

On the central level of the house are an open-plan kitchen, living and dining area, all benefiting from panoramic views of the trees and water. There's even an impressive view of the water from the ensuite to the main bedroom. 'Providing water views from every vantage point was an important part of the brief,' says Charles.

Timber features extensively in the interior of the home. Recycled timber was used for the flooring in the dining area, extending to the outdoor terrace. There is also extensive timber joinery, such as a credenza built into the living area. 'It's a fairly robust house. If it's not built-in, then it's extremely solid,' says Charles, referring to the chunky timber table in the dining area.

On the lowest level, designed with separate access, are two additional bedrooms, a bathroom, a billiard room and gymnasium. There is also a second living area. 'The two floor plates are almost identical. The two areas can be used in their entirety or partially closed down if the owners come down on their own,' says Charles.

Photography by Axiom Photography + Design

1   Entry
2   Study
3   Kitchen
4   Dining
5   Living
6   Bar
7   Bedroom
8   Dressing
9   Games
10 Laundry
11 Gymnasium

Lower level floor plan

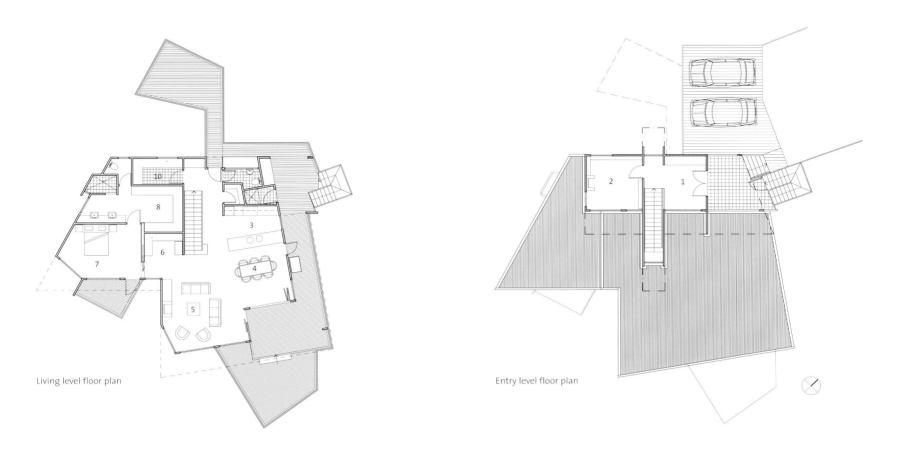

Living level floor plan

Entry level floor plan

207

Bed and Breakfast

ARCHITECT   LEIGH   WOOLLEY

'The focus is on the coastal dunes and the she-oaks.'

This beach house on the Freycinet Peninsula, on Tasmania's east coast, was conceived as a contemporary-style 'bed and breakfast'. Designed for a retired couple, the brief to architect Leigh Woolley was for two separate but linked pavilions, one for the owners, the other for guests.

While the brief was straightforward, the steep site provided a challenge. 'It's a relatively compact site (approximately 850 square metres). The program included accommodation for several people, parking for four cars, as well as a waste treatment area,' says Woolley, who received several tourism awards for this project.

As the site is reasonably steep, with an approximately 25-degree slope, the fall provided the area Woolley was looking for. The two separate pavilions, joined by a glazed breezeway, enjoy views over Great Oyster Bay. 'I didn't want the building to appear too prominent on the site. The focus is on the coastal dunes and the she-oaks,' says Woolley. To minimise the impact of the building and evoke the colours of the landscape, Woolley selected materials such as white concrete block and shadow-clad grooved plywood, painted grey.

The owners' pavilion includes a kitchen, living and dining area, together with two bedrooms and a bathroom. There is also a large private deck for the owners to enjoy. The guest quarters, including three double bedrooms, ensuites, a separate sitting area and an outdoor deck are equally spacious. The two pavilions are slightly offset to create a protected courtyard space at the entry and front of the property.

Photography by Leigh Woolley

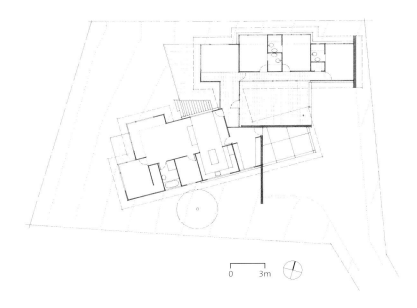

A Touch of the South Pacific

WALTER BARDA DESIGN

'They wanted the sense of an island home.'

This house in Whale Beach, on Sydney's northern beaches, has a slightly worn feel to it. Unlike the crisp white homes along the coastline, it merges into the landscape. 'It has quite a rustic feel. The colours and materials are recessive,' says architect Walter Barda.

Designed for a couple with three children, the brief was for something with a touch of the South Pacific. 'The owners had been living in Brazil for several years and they travel extensively. They wanted the sense of an island home,' says Barda.

As the house is on a steep site, the land was prepared for a multi-level house (six levels in total). Considerable excavation was required to maximise the site, as well as the view. 'There are water views from most rooms,' says Barda, who was also keen to create a large outdoor terrace from the living areas.

To accommodate the slope, the house runs vertically rather than horizontally. Stairs lead from ground level to a guest bedroom, bathroom, home office and gymnasium. While there are glimpses of the water from this level, the heroic vista is from the kitchen and living areas on the level above, which also features a large outdoor terrace and corner lanai.

To accentuate the view, Barda created a double-height space over the living areas. Complete with exposed timber trusses and a massive stone fireplace, there's a sense of rustic grandeur. During the warmer weather, the large timber and glass sliding doors can be pulled back and highlight louvred glass windows opened. 'The design lends itself to outdoor dining. But there's also the pavilion for less ideal weather,' says Barda.

Three levels were designed above the living areas. On the first level are the three children's bedrooms, together with a shared bathroom. A half level up is a mezzanine level, overlooking the living areas, used for watching television or simply reading. The main bedroom, ensuite and study are on the highest level. There is also a terrace with a swimming pool leading from this bedroom.

The materials chosen for the house are subtle and quite dark. Apart from the sandstone plinth, there is extensive use of timber, both new and recycled. Recycled timber posts feature prominently on a terrace and are overscaled in height and diameter. Shadow-clad timber also features, along with weatherboards. 'The house isn't supposed to look as though it was just built,' says Barda. The owners made their own contribution to the material selection, finding some used timber on the side of the road. 'We incorporated that timber into the kitchen joinery after dressing it,' says Barda.

Photography by Robert Morehead

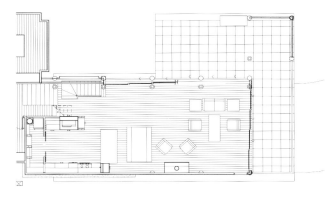

Living room level

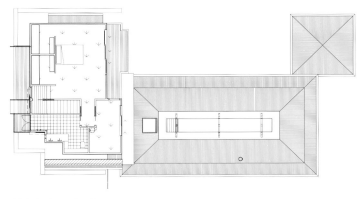

Main bedroom level

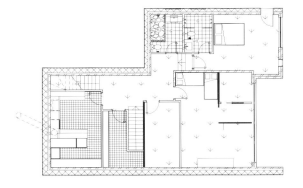

Playroom level

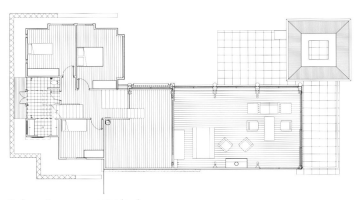

Bedroom/upper mezzanine level

Turned Around

P H O R M   A R C H I T E C T U R E   +   D E S I G N

'It's like unpacking a suitcase.'

This beach house at Seaforth, Queensland, needed to be completely reoriented, away from the heat of the western sun. Built in the 1960s, it was literally a hot-house. 'The heat was overwhelming. There was no escape!' says architect Paul Hotston, director of Phorm Architecture + Design.

As the budget was fairly modest, Hotston recycled the original house in the design. The house was reoriented away from its western aspect and repositioned within the site. A new kitchen was inserted and the verandahs were extended. As the house was designed for a couple with adult children, the owners and architect felt additional bedrooms were required (the original house had only two bedrooms). The original house was raised and a new bunk room was inserted at ground level. 'The owners often come here on their own. But at Christmas time, the house fills up with their children and their friends,' says Hotston.

One of the most dramatic changes to the house was a new two-storey beach tower, sited at the front of the property. Joined to the original house via a staircase and covered outdoor deck, the beach tower creates a contemporary front to the house. Made of Eco-plywood, expressed steel frame and featuring external louvres, this

wing comprises an outdoor beach room at ground level and an enclosed main bedroom and ensuite at the first level. 'The owners don't have to deal with a large beach house. They arrive, park their boat and unpack,' says Hotston. 'They don't need to use the entire house,' he adds, pointing out the most used path, between the outdoor beach room and the kitchen.

The main bedroom now enjoys views over the dunes to the Whitsunday coast. And even if the house has been locked up for a few weeks, it cools down a few minutes after arrival. 'It's like unpacking a suitcase,' says Hotston.

Photography by Jon Linkins

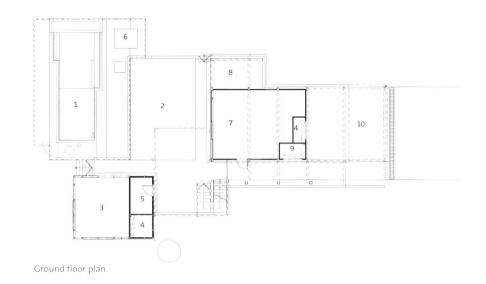

Ground floor plan

First floor plan

1	Pool	10	Garage
2	Courtyard	11	Deck
3	Beach room	12	Kitchen
4	Store	13	Bathroom
5	Bath house	14	Dining
6	Spa	15	Bedroom 2
7	Bunkhouse	16	Bedroom 3
8	Washdown	17	Sunroom
9	Laundry		

A New Life

S T U D I O   1 0 1   A R C H I T E C T S

'The Rheinzink captures the colour of the landscape.'

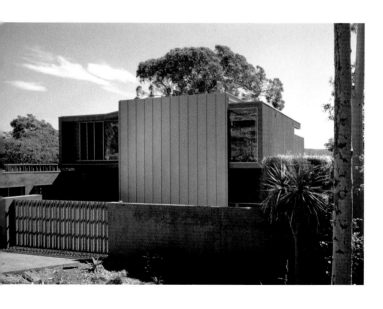

It's difficult to reconcile this beach house at Lorne, Victoria, with its previous incarnation, a simple, single-storey beach shack that offered glimpses of Loutitt Bay. 'The house had been owned by the family for several years. A few minor alterations had been made, such as the upgrade of the kitchen,' says architect Peter Woolard, director of Studio 101 Architects.

Owned by a couple with two adult children, the brief to the architects was to maximise views to the north, aligned to the bay. They also wanted to integrate the indoor and outdoor spaces, particularly as the land slopes 5 metres down from the road at the front of the property. 'Our clients also asked for a separate living area for their children, a place where they could entertain friends,' says Woolard.

Initial client discussions centred on retaining the original house and extending it. 'We thought about knocking it over completely. But the existing footprint set up the planning parameters. If we started from scratch, we might have been required to build further down the site, thereby reducing the water views,' says Woolard.

The original freestanding garage, located to one side of the house, was converted into a living area for the two children. Floor-to-ceiling glass doors were inserted in the garage's north wall, leading to a new timber deck. A kitchenette and a bathroom were also included in the new quarters.

Substantial changes were made to the original house. The ground and only floor of the original home was completely reworked. It now comprises four bedrooms, including the main bedroom with ensuite, a bathroom and a separate powder room. The bathrooms are clearly delineated with recycled timber battens, which also form a feature wall for a new staircase.

The new first floor is also clearly delineated. Constructed in timber, the first floor is adorned with Rheinzink panels. 'The Rheinzink captures the colour of the landscape. The ribs in the zinc cast their own shadows on the house,' says Woolard, who was also keen to reduce the scale of the first-floor addition.

Upstairs, there is a large open-plan kitchen, living and dining area, flanked to the north by floor-to-ceiling glass doors and windows. And to attract additional light, highlight windows wrap around the living areas. And rather than glimpses of water through tree trunks, there are panoramic views from numerous vantage points, both inside and on the terraces outside the home.

Photography by Trevor Mein

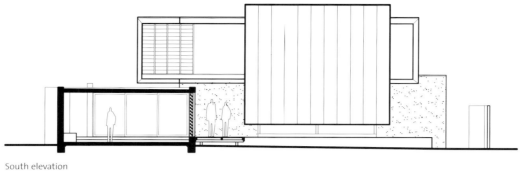

South elevation

North elevation

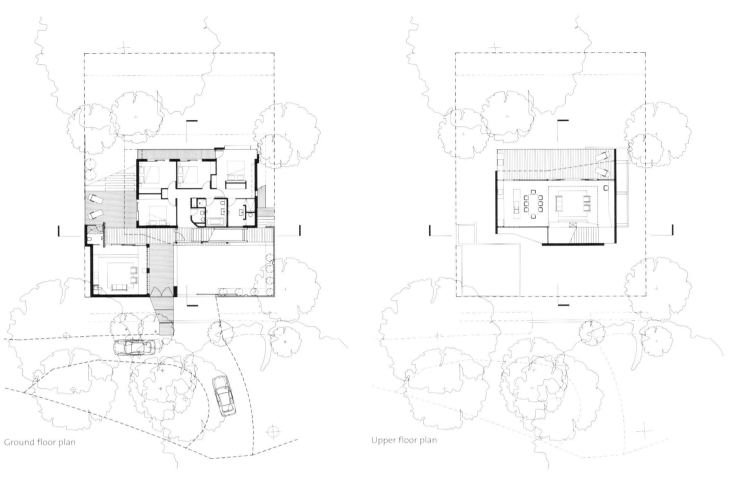

Ground floor plan

Upper floor plan

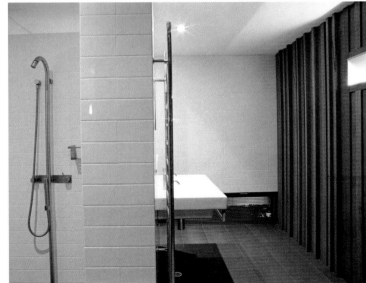

The Letter K

A S H T O N   R A G G A T T   M c D O U G A L L

'Our clients enjoyed seeing these esoteric designs.'

This house, on Victoria's Bellarine Peninsula, was designed by Ashton Raggatt McDougall Architects (ARM) for clients who wanted something challenging. 'The owners weren't afraid of new concepts. They embrace new ideas,' says architect Howard Raggatt, one of three directors of ARM, who worked closely with project architect Sophie Cleland.

The owners, a couple with two grown children, had few requirements in their brief to the architects. There was a request for separation between adults and children as well as a separate study and generous bookshelves for the owners' significant collection of books.

Given carte blanche to experiment, ARM came up with the letter K as a possible form for the new beach house. 'There are two parts to a design. One is to respond to a brief and the owners' needs, together with looking at the site. The other is creating a strategy that will tease out some of the more complex ideas,' says Raggatt.

The ground level, comprising the home's 'shadowy' base, is made of concrete block work and partially clad in dark grey timber. The first floor appears slightly lighter, constructed of timber and painted a lighter shade of grey. As striking as the building's jagged edges are flashes of red beneath the soffit and ceiling to the carport and undercroft.

While vibrant red is restrained on the exterior due to local planning guidelines, it's expressed within the home, both at ground level and on the upper levels. The ground floor includes a carport, also used as a covered outdoor area, two bedrooms, a bathroom, cellar, storeroom and a home cinema.

A staircase leads to the first floor, with its extraordinary bright red K-shaped bookshelf, which forms a wall as well as part of the balustrade. Integral to the 17-metre-long open-plan living, dining and kitchen area, MDF gloss shelving creates an entirely new concept for arranging books. The bookshelves in the main bedroom are just as novel. Forming a bedhead and allowing the letter K to be expressed as a bedside table, there seem to be no limits to how a bookshelf can be designed. 'Our clients enjoyed seeing these esoteric designs. Many people have difficulty looking at quite abstract ideas,' says Raggatt, who included suspended bookshelves in the study, accessed via a spiral staircase adjacent to the kitchen.

ARM's K house is more than the representation of an interesting letter in the alphabet; it a dynamic beach house, with easy access to the beach and shaped to shelter the owners from the wind.

Photography by Peter Bennetts

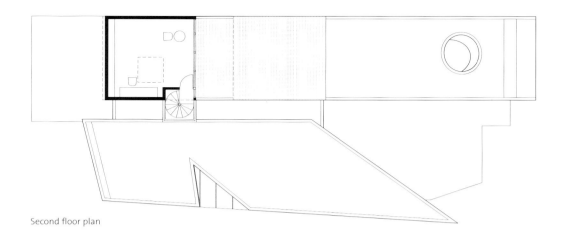

Second floor plan

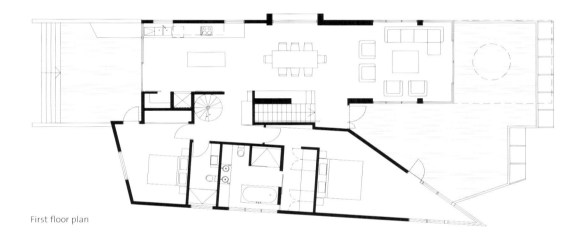

First floor plan

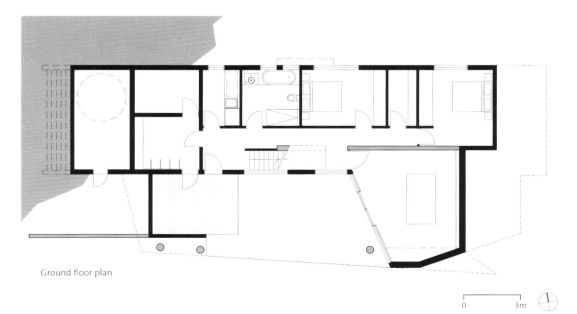

Ground floor plan

0   3m

Glimpses of Water

LUIGI ROSSELLI ARCHITECTS

'We wanted to orient the house to the views, but also take in the light.'

This house, designed by architect Luigi Rosselli, enjoys glimpses of the water. Only a short walk to the beach, the original cottage focused mainly on the large house next door. 'The cottage wasn't large enough for a family with three small children,' says Rosselli.

A two-storey house, with basement car parking and storage below has replaced the cottage. 'The site is reasonably small (approximately 300 square metres). We wanted to ensure there was sufficient garden for the children to play in,' says Rosselli, whose brief also included a swimming pool.

The house is constructed in stone, rendered brick, timber and glass. A sandstone fence anchors the building to the site, which slopes towards the south. 'We wanted to orient the house to the views (south), but also take in the light,' says Rosselli, who was also keen to remove the focus from the house next door.

Rosselli created an internal lightwell in the centre of the house. A sculptural staircase features a large skylight directly above, as well as a picture window at the top of the stairs. 'With this lightwell, there was less reliance on a northern vista,' he says.

On the ground floor are the kitchen, living and dining areas, which open up to the stairwell/light core. There is also a playroom for the children, as well as a separate study. And on the first floor are four bedrooms, with the main bedroom connected to a large terrace overlooking the pool. The terrace of this bedroom provides a canopy for the outdoor eating area adjacent to the pool.

To modulate the light on the first floor, and to reduce the scale of the house, Rosselli used timber for the walls, as well as for the adjustable shutters. To ensure the children are always in sight, Rosselli designed a curvaceous canteen-style window adjacent to the kitchen. 'The window reminds me of a captain's window in a ship. With three young children, it's not always the weather you need to watch out for,' he says.

Photography by Richard Glover

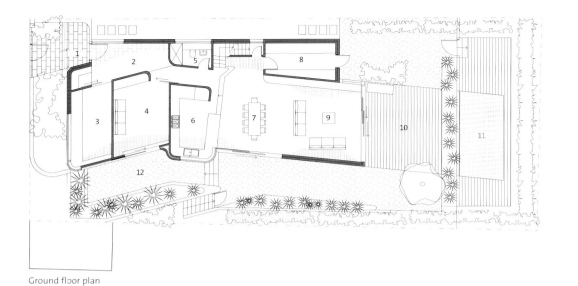

Ground floor plan

First floor plan

1	Porch	8	Laundry	15	Bedroom 2
2	Entry	9	Living room	16	Bathroom 2
3	Study	10	Deck	17	Bedroom 3
4	Playroom	11	Swimming pool	18	Dressing room
5	Bathroom 1	12	Roof garden	19	Master bedroom
6	Kitchen	13	Balcony 1	20	Ensuite
7	Dining room	14	Bedroom 1	21	Balcony 2

Controlling the Views

B. E.   A R C H I T E C T U R E

'We've tried to personalise each view, whether it's from the living areas, or from the main bedroom.'

This house at Flinders, on Victoria's Mornington Peninsula, is buried deep into its 4-hectare site. Invisible from the street, the cedar-clad house only appears at the end of a long winding driveway. 'We wanted to control the views over Bass Strait rather than present just one vista,' says designer Broderick Ely, director of B.E. Architecture.

Designed for a couple with two adult children, the brief was to create a large house with a focus on entertaining. 'It's almost two interconnected houses,' says Ely, referring to the separate guest accommodation comprising three bedrooms and a living area with its own kitchenette.

However, it is the main pavilion, with an open-plan kitchen and living area that draws the immediate accolades. Featuring 5-metre-high ceilings of painted timber and floor-to-ceiling glass windows and doors, there is a sense of connection to the rolling hills and Bass Strait in the distance. 'We've tried to personalise each view, whether it's from the living areas, or from the main bedroom,' says Ely.

The main bedroom, conceived as a separate two-storey wing, is linked to the living areas via an enclosed breezeway. On the first floor are the main bedroom, ensuite and dressing area. Below is a cabana/gymnasium that leads directly to the swimming pool. However, rather than elevate the pool, it is positioned below a 35-metre-long stone wall. 'You really only see the pool when you lean over the rock wall. We didn't want it to detract from the larger vista,' says Ely, who also used the stone wall to create a plinth for the covered terraces above.

Four outdoor terraces create a series of informal rooms around the house. Featuring cypress posts and a polycarbonate roof lined with timber, these outdoor terraces merge with indoor spaces.

While the house is contemporary, inspiration was drawn from rustic buildings built in America in the 1920s. 'I visited the library in Colorado. In one of the books I picked up were old photos of buildings constructed in rough stonework,' says Ely, who wanted to include similar textures in this Australian house.

Photography by Trevor Mein

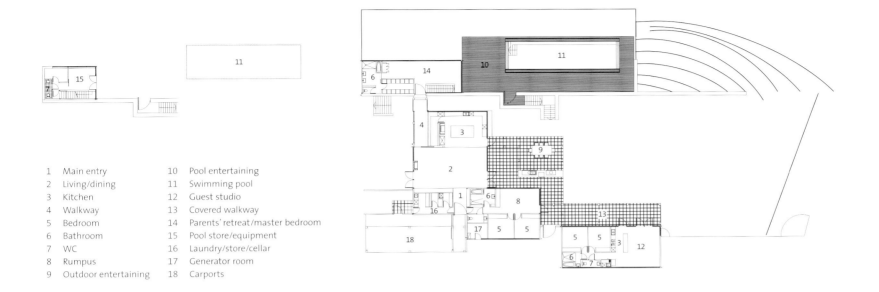

1 Main entry
2 Living/dining
3 Kitchen
4 Walkway
5 Bedroom
6 Bathroom
7 WC
8 Rumpus
9 Outdoor entertaining

10 Pool entertaining
11 Swimming pool
12 Guest studio
13 Covered walkway
14 Parents' retreat/master bedroom
15 Pool store/equipment
16 Laundry/store/cellar
17 Generator room
18 Carports

Orua Bay

MOLLER ARCHITECTS

'It's a simple and dramatic plan.'

This house takes in the spectacular views of Manukau Harbour, on the west coast of New Zealand's North Island. Nestled in the native coastal vegetation, the beach house is a clear expression of the materials used: weathered cedar, glass and steel. 'The house is designed to respect the hillside environment. The full-height glazing and large overhangs ensure an even-tempered interior,' says architect Gordon Moller. 'We were also keen to ensure passive solar gain during the winter months as well as controlling glare from the summer sun,' he adds.

As the site is relatively steep, the design includes two levels at the rear. 'It's a simple and dramatic plan, essentially rectangular in form, with a 6-metre void above the living space,' says Moller.

At ground level are the open-plan kitchen, living and dining areas, with the first-floor bedrooms forming a 'canopy' over the kitchen. The first floor also creates a sense of intimacy in the living area. On the ground floor, steel beams and columns delineate the open space, as does a bridge forming a link from the two bedrooms upstairs to the external deck, the latter 'punching' out to maximise harbour views.

Moller Architects also designed a separate garage and third bedroom to the uphill side of the house. This separate pavilion creates a courtyard between the two buildings, an ideal place to go in more inclement weather. Protection is provided on the main deck, with a cantilevered balcony extending almost past the edge of the deck.

As the bedrooms overlook the living areas, floor-to-ceiling moveable cedar shutters are included in each bedroom. These can be closed at night, or pulled back to enjoy the harbour views. The arrangement also creates an informal ambience in the house, with those upstairs being able to communicate with those sitting in the living areas.

Photography by Gordon Moller

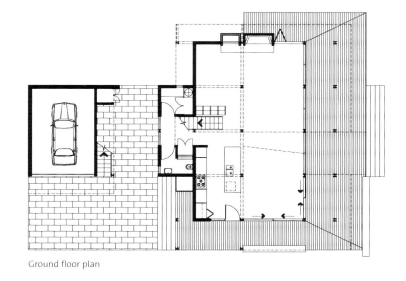

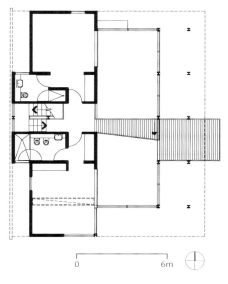

Ground floor plan

First floor plan

0   6m

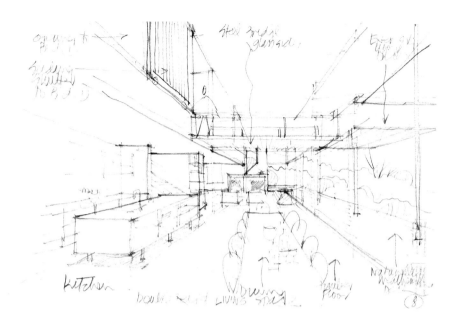

Balinese Influence

BLIGH VOLLER NIELD ARCHITECTURE

'Essentially, it's one large verandah.'

Located on the Sunshine Coast, Queensland, this house has a strong Balinese influence. Positioned at the end of a cul-de-sac on an established canal estate, the house features its own private beach. The house was designed for a couple, one of whom spent considerable time travelling through Southeast Asia. 'The brief included a sense of his travels, but he didn't want a pastiche reproduction piece,' says architect Shane Thompson.

While the house appears completely new, it was built on the foundations of a 1970s Spanish mission-style house. Some original walls were incorporated, but the original house has been extended considerably. The two-storey house now includes three wings, interspersed with six bodies of water.

The first body of water is experienced in the front courtyard, where a bridge links the gate to the entrance. At the front of the house (facing the street) is a two-storey wing with a guest bedroom and garage. Above the garage and bedroom are four additional bedrooms, together with bathrooms. 'The owners' children are grown up, but they regularly stay, along with their children. And there are also overseas guests,' says Thompson.

Past this wing is a large two-storey reception area, offering views over a pond to the swimming pool and the river beyond. This central courtyard, with pond, contains a Balinese sculpture. 'The spaces are essentially organised around this courtyard,' says Thompson, gesturing towards the two additional wings. One of these wings comprises a series of sitting areas, with the main bedroom and ensuite above. The third wing is given over to the kitchen and living areas. The outdoor living areas, with generous canopied outdoor rooms, are further important elements of the design.

There are elements in this home that are derivative of a Balinese house. The ceilings throughout the house feature woven raffia mats, bought in Bali in a street market. Yet, while there are Asian touches, there's also a contemporary feel to this home, with large timber and glass doors disappearing into cavity walls. 'Essentially, it's one large verandah,' says Thompson. 'The spaces are informal. Here it's about stripping away inhibitions and relaxing by the pool or the river,' he adds.

Photography by David Sandison and
Neil 'Moonwalker' Armstrong

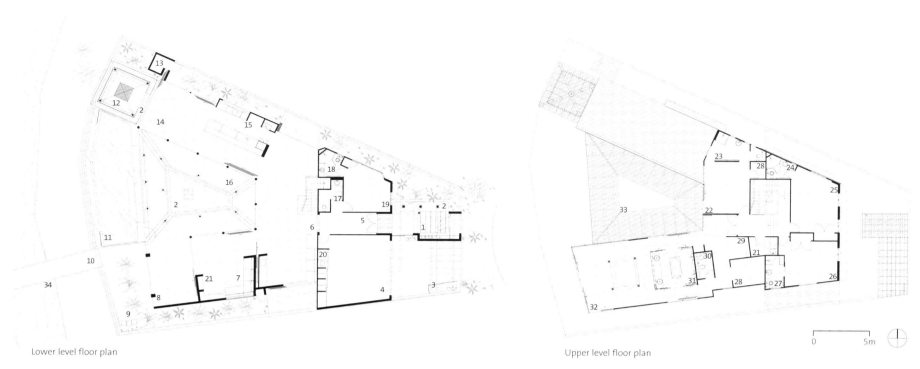

Lower level floor plan   Upper level floor plan

0   5m

1	Gatehouse	8	Lanai	15	Kitchen	22	Bedroom 4	29	Study
2	Pond	9	Outdoor shower	16	Arcaded court	23	Bathroom 4	30	WC
3	Storage	10	Jetty	17	Powder room	24	Bathroom 2	31	Ensuite
4	Garage	11	Pool	18	Bathroom 1	25	Bedroom 2	32	Master bedroom
5	Entry	12	Bale	19	Bedroom 1	26	Bedroom 3	33	Void
6	Hall	13	Pool equipment	20	Laundry	27	Bathroom 3	34	Canal
7	Lounge	14	Dining	21	Fireplace	28	Walk-in robe		

Tropical Treehouse

CARR DESIGN GROUP

'I also wanted the house to have a lush tropical feel, where walls and doors are quite transparent.'

Nick Carr, a director of the Carr Design Group, wasn't sure what he was going to do with vacant land purchased at Port Douglas, in Far North Queensland. While the 1000-square-metre site could have accommodated one house, he decided on building two, selling one and keeping the other for himself as a holiday house.

Located on Flagstaff Hill, a few minutes' walk from the town centre, the two houses are almost identical. Made of steel, glass and timber, each features a textured concrete wall (also the joining wall). 'We didn't want to conceal the "bones" of the houses,' says Carr, referring to the 4.5-metre-wide grid system used in the construction.

Carr worked closely with architects Mat Wright and Amy Muir, both of Carr Design. 'I wanted something that was fairly low maintenance. A place that could be as quickly "opened up" as "closed down",' says Carr, referring to the timber shutters that frame the house. 'I also wanted the house to have a lush tropical feel, where walls and doors are quite transparent,' he adds.

While the house appears relatively compact from the street, the façade conceals three levels (there is a fall in the land of 4.5 metres). The kitchen and living areas occupy the central level, together with an exterior elevated dining area.

There is also a bedroom and ensuite on this level. On the top level are the main bedroom and ensuite opening to an internal courtyard. And on the lowest level are a bedroom, ensuite and separate laundry, with this bedroom overlooking a swimming pool.

Although the house is relatively narrow – approximately 6 metres – it feels considerably larger. The galley-style kitchen is to one side of the living area and the outdoor spaces are integral to the design. 'The main bedroom is positioned in line with the tree canopies. You feel like you're sleeping in the trees,' says Carr.

Photography by Peter Bennetts

Level one floor plan

Level two floor plan

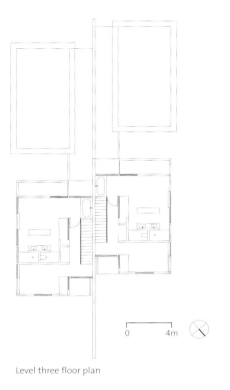

0   4m

Level three floor plan

Alfresco Living

'*There's nothing better than just lying on the lounges and gazing out to the beach.*'

The owners of this beach house live on a farm in Hawkes Bay, on the east coast of New Zealand's North Island. 'Our clients wanted a place near the beach, where family could come together on weekends and holidays,' says architect Brent Hulena.

Southern Hawkes Bay is a comfortable 45-minute drive from the owner's home, but the coastal environment couldn't be more different. The hilly terrain is as dramatic as the surf beach. 'It's quite a desolate area. There are only a handful of houses,' says Hulena.

Although the children have left home, the brief was for a house with five bedrooms. 'There are also grandchildren on the scene,' says Hulena, who was asked to create one large living area where all the family could congregate.

As a consequence, the concrete (block), steel and glass house is designed in an L-shape. One wing, facing the water, comprises a 15-metre open-plan kitchen, dining and living area. Beyond the kitchen door are two bedrooms and a library. The shorter side of the L features another two bedrooms, one of which is used as a bunkroom that doubles as a second living area for grandchildren.

As the region can experience extreme winds, the architects designed two outdoor areas, one leading from the living areas to the beach on the east, the other to the west. The western courtyard is not only protected from the wind, but also benefits from views through the generous glazing on either side of the kitchen and living areas through to the beach beyond.

To strengthen the link between the indoors and outdoors, all the rooms open onto outdoor areas. When it comes to alfresco dining, bi-folding windows were incorporated in the kitchen, enabling easy entertaining to the eastern terrace. A fireplace in the western courtyard allows for comfortable evening dining. 'The house is used year-round, so it was important to create comfortable outdoor spaces,' says Hulena.

While the outdoors and indoors are blurred in this home, the living spaces are pivotal to the design. 'There's nothing better than just lying on the lounges and gazing out to the beach,' says Hulena, who included aluminium louvres above the glass doors in the living areas, as well as over the outdoor terrace, to control sunlight.

Photography by Kallan MacLeod

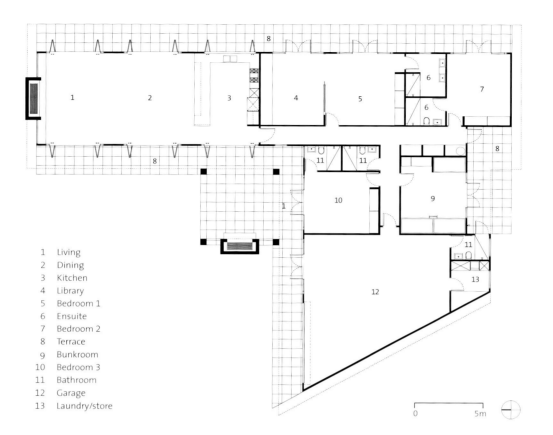

1 Living
2 Dining
3 Kitchen
4 Library
5 Bedroom 1
6 Ensuite
7 Bedroom 2
8 Terrace
9 Bunkroom
10 Bedroom 3
11 Bathroom
12 Garage
13 Laundry/store

0   5m

High on a Hill

I R E D A L E   P E D E R S E N   H O O K   A R C H I T E C T S

'The only things visible are the sand and ocean.'

This beach house in Perth, Western Australia has had several incarnations. Originally built in the 1970s, the brown brick house featured raked ceilings and high clerestory windows. With the 1980s and the postmodern movement, the beach house was given a makeover. 'The bricks were rendered and painted salmon pink. The ceilings were also lowered, concealing the angled roof lines,' says architect Adrian Iredale.

The brief was to renovate the house while extending the living areas to maximise views of the Indian Ocean. While the panoramic vistas are impressive, so is the glare and heat generated from the western elevation. The architects 'pushed' the living areas beyond the original footprint and created a generous steel eave over the new deck. 'We stayed away from the typical skillion-shaped roof, orienting the eaves downwards rather than towards the sky,' says Iredale.

'It began with the memory of the Danish architect Jørn Utzon's sketch of dense rolling clouds over inhabited platforms. The new roof takes on the form of an overscaled 'cap', responding to the intensity of the sun, wind and rain,' says Iredale.

The new sections in the house are articulated by steel, leaving no doubt as to what was added in the most recent renovation. Along with the extension of the living areas, the house was entirely renovated. A new kitchen was installed, along with new bathrooms. The original raked ceilings were also unveiled in the process, allowing natural light to again descend on the spaces. Balconies were added to the living spaces as well as the main bedroom.

While there is a highway separating the house from the beach, the site benefits from being perched high on a hill, well above the sight of moving traffic. 'From the living areas, you can't see the traffic. The only things visible are the sand and ocean,' says Iredale.

Photography by Shannon McGrath and Andrew Pritchard

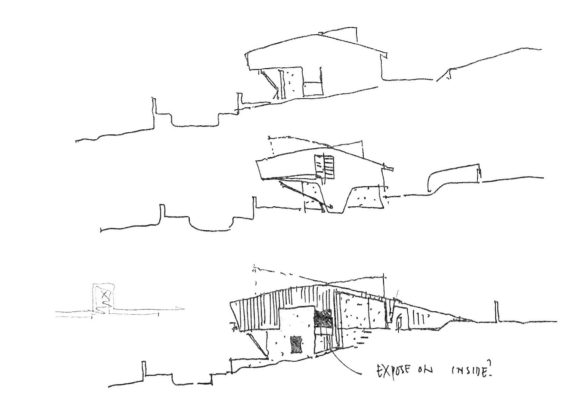

EXPOSE ON INSIDE?

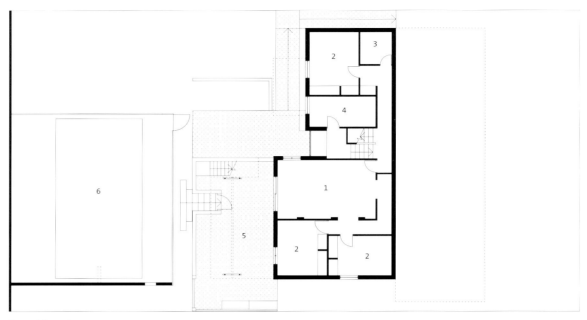

Ground floor plan

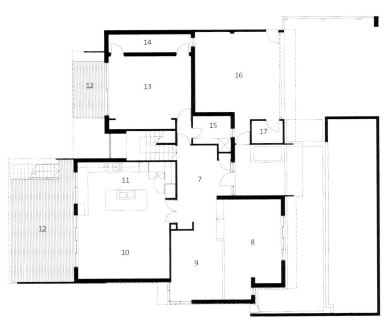

1   Games room
2   Bedroom
3   Bathroom
4   Laundry/WC
5   Terrace
6   Pool
7   Entry
8   Lounge
9   Dining
10 Family
11 Kitchen
12 Timber deck
13 Bedroom
14 Clothes store
15 Bathroom
16 Garage
17 Store

0   5m

First floor plan

Nestled in the Dunes

KERSTIN THOMPSON ARCHITECTS

'The two arms capture the natural light, as well as forming protection from the western sun and strong winds.'

This house at Blairgowrie, on Victoria's Mornington Peninsula, doesn't have sea views. Surrounded by dense tea-trees and coastal scrub, the house resonates a sense of calm. Nestled in the dunes, the house feels remote.

Designed for a couple with three children, the single-storey fibro-cement house occupies one half of a double block. Conceived as two wings, the house sits at the base of a bowl-shaped impression. 'The two arms capture the natural light, as well as forming protection from the western sun and strong winds,' says architect Kerstin Thompson.

To increase protection from both sun and wind, the children's wing is raised above the main living wing. The floor of the living areas was sunk into the ground, allowing for a seat at the edge of the living areas to be used both indoors and out. 'We wanted to connect the living spaces to the courtyard. We also wanted to create a strong anchoring point,' says Thompson.

The longer and narrower of the two wings comprises the children's bedrooms, together with shared bathroom facilities. And unlike most conventional houses, there is no corridor, simply gently graded steps and sliding doors between the four bedrooms. 'This wing is like a large bunkroom,' says Thompson, who included separate doors to the terrace. 'When the children get older, they'll want more privacy,' she adds.

In contrast to the main living wing, the children's wing features hoop pine walls and plywood floors. 'We wanted to create a division, not just with function, but with the materials used.'

One of the core areas in the house is the indoor–outdoor room, or 'breezeway'. Framed by sliding perforated steel doors on either side, the breezeway can be used as an enclosed play area for the children during the colder months. During the warmer months, this area is more akin to a verandah.

Photography by Jeremy The

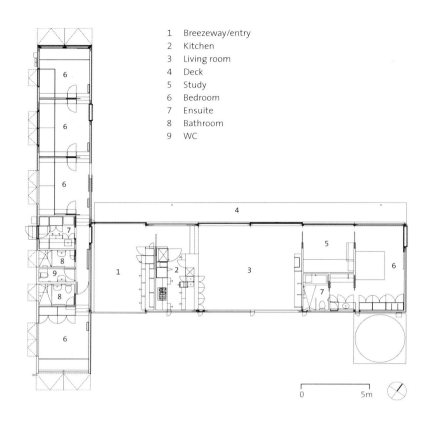

1 Breezeway/entry
2 Kitchen
3 Living room
4 Deck
5 Study
6 Bedroom
7 Ensuite
8 Bathroom
9 WC

0   5m

Architect contact details

ARCHITEKTUR
11a Calder Place
Glendowie, Auckland
New Zealand
+64 9 575 1603
architektur.co.nz

ASHTON RAGGATT MCDOUGALL
Level 11, 522 Flinders Lane
Melbourne Vic 3000
Australia
+61 3 9629 1222
a-r-m.com.au

BAILEY ARCHITECTS
108 Park Road
Newmarket, Auckland
New Zealand
+64 9 377 4361
baileyarchitects.co.nz

BARK DESIGN ARCHITECTS
Studio 185, Sunshine Road
Tinbeerwah Qld 4563
Australia
+61 7 5471 0340
barkdesign.com.au

B.E. ARCHITECTURE
16 Cecil Place
Prahran Vic 3181
Australia
+61 3 9529 6433
bearchitecture.com

BELLEMO & CAT
23a Eastment Street
Northcote Vic 3070
Australia
+61 3 9489 5812
www.bellemocat.com

BERNARD SEEBER ARCHITECTS
152 High Street
Fremantle WA 6160
Australia
+61 8 9336 2655
bernardseeber.com

BIRD DE LA COEUR ARCHITECTS
66 Market Street
Southbank Vic 3006
Australia
+61 3 9682 4566
bdlc.com.au

BKK ARCHITECTS
Level 9, 180 Russell Street
Melbourne Vic 3000
Australia
+61 3 9671 4555
b-k-k.com.au

BLIGH VOLLER NIELD ARCHITECTURE
365 St Pauls Terrace
Fortitude Valley Qld 4006
Australia
+61 7 3852 2525
bvn.com.au

BURO ARCHITECTURE + INTERIORS
Level 1, 389 Lonsdale Street
Melbourne Vic 3000
Australia
+61 3 9670 1966
buroarchitects.com.au

CARR DESIGN GROUP
Level 4/31 Flinders Lane
Melbourne Vic 3000
Australia
+61 3 9654 8692
carr.net.au

Casey Brown Architecture

Level 1, 63 William Street

East Sydney NSW 2010

Australia

+61 2 9360 7977

caseybrown.com.au

Centrum Architects

37 South Caroline Street

South Yarra Vic 3141

Australia

+61 3 9821 4644

charles@centrum.com.au

Chenchow Little Pty Ltd

Suite 3, 151 Foveaux Street

Surry Hills NSW 2010

Australia

+61 2 9357 4333

chenchowlittle.com

Cox Rayner

Level 2, 2 Edward Street

Brisbane Qld 4000

Australia

+61 7 3210 0844

cox.com.au

Daniel Marshall Architect

Level 6, 16 High Street

Auckland 1001

New Zealand

+64 9 302 3661

marshall-architect.co.nz

Hayne Wadley Architects

78 Charles Street

Northcote Vic 3070

Australia

+61 3 9482 2865

haynewadley.com.au

Hulena Architects

9 Melrose Street

Newmarket, Auckland

New Zealand

+64 9 524 6955

hulena.com

Iredale Pedersen Hook Architects

Murray Mews, 329-331 Murray Street

Perth WA 6000

Australia

+61 8 9322 9750

iredalepedersenhook.com

ITN Architects

Level 2/184 Brunswick Street

Fitzroy Vic 3065

Australia

+61 3 9416 3883

itnarchitects.com

Jackson Clements Burrows

One Harwood Place

Melbourne Vic 3000

Australia

+61 3 9654 6227

jcba.com.au

JAM Architects

7 Howard Street

Richmond Vic 3121

Australia

+61 3 9429 7744

jamarchitects.com.au

Kerstin Thompson Architects

54 Charles Street

Fitzroy Vic 3065

Australia

+61 3 9419 4969

kerstinthompson.com

Lahz Nimmo Architects

Level 5, 116-122 Kippax Street

Surry Hills NSW 2010

Australia

+61 2 9211 1220

lahznimmo.com

Leigh Woolley Architect

224 Murray Street

Hobart Tas 7000

Australia

+61 3 6231 1711

leighwoolley@ozemail.com.au

Luigi Rosselli Architects

15 Randle Street

Surry Hills NSW 2010

Australia

+61 2 9281 1498

luigirosselli.com

Marcus O'Reilly Architects

19 Baker Street

St Kilda Vic 3182

Australia

+61 3 9534 3715

marcusoreilly.com

McBride Charles Ryan

4/21 Wynnstay Road

Prahran Vic 3181

Australia

+61 3 9510 1006

mcbridecharlesryan.com.au

Moller Architects

Level 13 West Plaza, 3 Albert Street

Auckland

New Zealand

+64 9 357 0686

www.mollerarchitects.com

Paul Morgan Architects

Level 10, 221 Queen Street

Melbourne Vic 3000

Australia

+61 3 9600 3255

paulmorganarchitects.com

Phorm Architecture + Design

6 /173 Boundary Street

West End Qld 4101

Australia

+61 7 3255 2733

phorm@optusnet.com.au

Richard Kerr Architecture

The Edge Studio, 14 Jordan Street

Malvern Vic 3144

Australia

+61 3 9090 7460

rkarch.com.au

Robert Andary Architecture

PO Box 1805

Subiaco WA 6904

Australia

+61 8 9367 1336

ra.architecture.net.au

Sally Draper Architects

72 McKean Street

North Fitzroy Vic 3068

Australia

+61 3 9486 6606

sdraper@sallydraperarchitects.com.au

Simon Rodrigues Architect

c/- Rodrigues Bodycoat Architects

575 Stirling Highway

Cottesloe WA 6011

Australia

+61 8 9286 3304

simon.r@rba.architecture.net.au

SIMON SWANEY

c/- Bates Smart

243 Liverpool Street

East Sydney NSW 2010

Australia

+61 2 8354 5100

sswaney@batessmart.com

SJB ARCHITECTS

25 Coventry Street

Melbourne Vic 3000

Australia

+61 3 9699 6688

sjb.com.au

SODAA

Unit 3 140 Onslow Road

Shenton Park WA 6006

Australia

+61 8 9388 6400

sodaa.com.au

SORENSEN ARCHITECTS

204 Rosa Brook Road

Margaret River WA 6285

Australia

+61 8 9757 3581

sorensenarchitects.com.au

STRACHAN GROUP ARCHITECTS

Studio 2b, 2b Empire Road

Epsom, Auckland

New Zealand

+64 9 638 6302

sgaltd.co.nz

STUDIO 101 ARCHITECTS

1 Dennys Place

Geelong Vic 3220

Australia

+61 3 5221 9131

studio101.com.au

WALTER BARDA DESIGN

38 Hardie Street

Darlinghurst NSW 2010

Australia

+61 2 9360 2340

enquiries@walterbardadesign.com

WOLVERIDGE ARCHITECTS

121 Rokeby Street

Collingwood Vic 3066

Australia

+61 3 9486 9882

wolveridge.com.au

WOODS BAGOT

Podium Level 1, 3 Southgate Avenue

Southbank Vic 3006

Australia

+61 3 8646 6600

woodsbagot.com.au

WRIGHT FELDHUSEN ARCHITECTS

4/245 Churchill Avenue

Subiaco WA 6904

Australia

+61 8 9388 7244

wrightfeldhusen.com

Acknowledgments

I would like to thank all the architects featured in this book, along with the owners of these homes in such superb beachside locations. Thanks must also go to the many photographers who contributed. Their images allow these wonderful projects to be fully appreciated. I would also like to thank my partner Naomi for her support and literary criticism.

Stephen Crafti

Additional photography credits:

Page 6

Architect: Centrum Architects

Photography by Axiom Photography + Design

Page 8

Architect: Jackson Clements Burrows Architects

Photography by John Gollings

Page 10

Architect: Walter Barda Architecture

Photography by Robert Morehead